KIDS
WHO
DID

Other books by Kirsty Murray

Zarconi's Magic Flying Fish
Market Blues
Walking Home with Marie-Claire
Vulture's Gate
India Dark
The Four Seasons of Lucy McKenzie
The Year It All Ended
Eat the Sky, Drink the Ocean (as editor)

CHILDREN OF THE WIND
Bridie's Fire
Becoming Billy Dare
A Prayer for Blue Delaney
The Secret Life of Maeve Lee Kwong

KIRSTY MURRAY

KIDS WHO DID

REAL KIDS WHO RULED, REBELLED, SURVIVED AND THRIVED

ALLEN&UNWIN
SYDNEY • MELBOURNE • AUCKLAND • LONDON

This revised and updated edition published by Allen & Unwin in 2019

First published by Allen & Unwin as *Tough Stuff* in 1999

Allen & Unwin
83 Alexander Street
Crows Nest NSW 2065
Australia
Phone: (61 2) 8425 0100
Email: info@allenandunwin.com
Web: www.allenandunwin.com

A catalogue record for this book is available from the National Library of Australia

ISBN 978 1 76052 447 0

For teaching resources, explore www.allenandunwin.com/resources/for-teachers

Cover and text design by Joanna Hunt
Cover and text illustrations by Kelly Canby
Set in 11.2 pt ITC Legacy Serif Book by Joanna Hunt
Printed in February 2019 by McPherson's Printing Group, Australia

10 9 8 7 6 5 4 3 2 1

kirstymurray.com

In 1999, I dedicated this book to Billy,
aka William Vyvyan Murray. Though he's now
a grown-up, he has always been a 'kid who did'.
For the 2019 edition, I dedicate every new story to
Louis Frances Henning, who is a 'kid who does'
and a continuing source of inspiration.

CONTENTS

INTRODUCTION

In 1999, I was proud to launch the first edition of *Tough Stuff: true stories about kids and courage*. It was a book I'd dreamt of writing all my life, and it was jam-packed full of stories about people who inspired me. Since then, some of the people whose stories were included in that collection have died. Others have continued to live amazing lives. When my publishers suggested I update the original stories for a new edition, I couldn't resist adding eleven new stories as well as revisiting the old ones. Inspiring kids are born every minute of every day.

These stories aren't about being famous. They're about kids who saved lives, came up with big ideas, survived terrible circumstances and believed they could make a difference. Not all of these stories have happy endings, and some of the children are still growing up so their futures are not yet written.

History is full of stories of kids who have done amazing things, but I picked the stories for this book because each of these children has shown incredible courage. The word 'courage' comes from the Latin word *cor* (heart). These kids faced some of the toughest challenges that any human being can confront, yet they stayed true to their heartfelt beliefs. Whether they lived or died, thrived or simply survived, the children in this book help us to understand the true meaning of courage.

RESCUERS

CHEATING DEATH, CHANGING FATE, SAVING LIVES

Coming to the rescue and especially saving a life makes you a hero in everyone's books – but being brave doesn't mean not being scared. Kid rescuers are ordinary kids who out of the blue did something extraordinary.

All the kids in this chapter won awards for their bravery, either from the government or from various organisations that give prizes for heroism. But the real prize for each of them was knowing that they saved someone's life.

BILLY AND THE BULL

Billy Corcoran was only nine years old, but he was already pretty useful around the farm that his family owned in Amphitheatre, Victoria. When his dad, Greg, asked him to help sort some cattle at a neighbour's farm, Billy was keen to go.

It was a windy day in the early spring of 1994. Late in the afternoon, Billy and Greg drove to the neighbour's cattle yard. Their job was to separate the bulls from the steers, so that the neighbour could send some away to be sold.

Greg sent Billy off to collect sticks to use in herding the cattle between pens. Then Greg climbed over the fence surrounding the cattle yard. When he opened a gate between the pens, a steer bumped against it and the gate slammed into Greg, hitting him hard in the back and making him stumble forward. A bull, alarmed by the sudden movement, charged the defenceless man as he lay on the ground.

Billy heard his dad shout and ran towards the yard.

'Watch out, Billy!' cried Greg as the huge bull bore down on top of him and rammed him with its head.

As Greg struggled to avoid the angry bull's hooves, he discovered he couldn't move his legs. He was paralysed from the waist down. In the same moment, Greg saw a flash of blond hair and realised Billy was racing towards him, inside the pen.

'Run, Billy. Get out, Billy. Get out of here!" he screamed.

But Billy had other ideas. He beat the bull across the back and head with his sticks, driving it away from his dad.

'You get out of here. Clear off!' Billy shouted, thrashing the bull as hard as he could.

When the bull withdrew, Billy handed a stick to Greg to protect himself with. He raced across the yard to open the gate, planning to drive the bull into a neighbouring pen. But the minute Billy's back was turned, the crazy animal set to again.

Billy was across the yard and on the attack in a flash. Like a mad bull-terrier he rushed at the huge beast, giving it a painful blow across its eye. Billy's head didn't even reach the top of the bull's back, but he attacked it so fiercely that the stick he was using splintered and broke in his hands.

The bull backed off at last and Billy herded it out of the yard with his hands, shouting and clapping to shoo it into the adjoining pen. Then he swung the gate shut and raced back to his dad.

Billy knelt down and rested a hand on his dad's shoulder.

'I can't move, Billy,' said Greg. 'I haven't got any feeling in my legs.'

'Don't worry, Dad. Everything will be okay,' said Billy. 'I'll take care of you.'

Billy had heard that after bad accidents people go into shock. Greg Corcoran's face was the colour of white ash, and Billy could see he was struggling with the pain.

Billy ran back to the car and grabbed the mobile phone from the front seat, plus a coat and blanket from the back. He draped the blanket over his dad and then crouched down beside him while he phoned his mum. Their conversation was brief. She would contact the ambulance and be over as quickly as she could. Meanwhile, Billy was in charge.

'You have to keep warm, Dad,' he said as he climbed under the blanket with him. 'A bloke came to our school and talked to us about hypothermia. When you've had an accident, your body gets really shocked and you get really cold. I know what I'm doing. I'm gonna give you lots of cuddles to warm you up.'

The rain came before help arrived. Billy checked out a nearby shed and found an old horse blanket. Using the sticks he had gathered, he built a shelter over Greg to keep the rain off and then he hopped back under the blankets to keep his dad warm.

It took over half an hour for help to arrive. After Billy's dad was loaded into the ambulance, Billy got behind the wheel of his father's car and drove it over to their neighbour's house, following his mum who was in the car ahead of him.

No one was as surprised as Billy when the newspaper reporters turned up on his doorstep and started making a fuss over him.

'So why did you do it, Billy?' they asked.

''Cause I love my dad,' he answered, amazed that grown-ups could ask such a stupid question.

Thanks to Billy, his father wasn't permanently injured by the bull. Greg spent ten days in hospital but recovered the use of his legs and returned to work on their farm in Amphitheatre. Billy was later given a bravery award by the Royal Humane Society.

Country kids are often pretty good at rescuing people – working in the great outdoors with their parents, driving tractors and handling machinery or animals means they're put to the test more often than city kids.

City kids don't get as many opportunities to get behind the wheel but the little girl in the next story decided to learn to drive in the nick of time.

THE ONLY GIRL IN AN EMERGENCY

Nine-year-old Tatum De Koning and her younger brother Teagan climbed into the back seat of their mum's Toyota Kluger and put on their seatbelts. The family had bought the second-hand car only five days ago and Tatum was still excited about travelling to school in their 'new' car.

It was just after 8.30 a.m. on 28 March 2011, a regular school day like any other. Tatum waved goodbye to her dad, Mario, as he jumped into his own car to head off to work. The next time Mario would see his daughter, he'd see her in a whole new light, because no one in the De Koning family would ever forget the events of that morning.

While Tatum gazed out the window at the streets of their home town of Wallan, Victoria, their mum, Karen, flicked on the car radio.

'That's my favourite song!' said Tatum and she started humming along to 'The Only Girl in the World' by Rihanna.

Karen turned the car into William Street, heading towards Wallan Primary School. Suddenly, the car sped up. Tatum saw her mum's hands fly off the wheel and bang against the side window.

'Mum!' said Tatum. 'What's wrong?' Then Tatum saw her mum's head jerk backwards.

Karen's eyes rolled back in her head as she was caught in the throes of a violent seizure. She had lost control of the car. As Karen's body stiffened, her foot jammed against the accelerator and the car spun out of control, travelling at over 100 kilometres per hour in a 60 zone.

The car sped into the lane of oncoming traffic and Tatum knew she had to move fast. As the car began to swerve, speeding towards a head-on collision, Tatum swiftly unbuckled her seatbelt and dived into the front seat. She leaned in front of her mum and grabbed hold of the steering wheel, pulling it hard to the left. Karen was still jammed behind the steering wheel so Tatum couldn't reach the brake pedal. Thanks to Tatum's quick thinking, the Kluger sped out of the path of the oncoming cars – but now it was careering towards a pole at top speed.

A long row of pine trees lined one side of the road. Tatum took a deep breath and steered the car towards the trees, clipping the branches at first, hoping the impact would help bring the car to a stop. Finally, the car slammed into the pine trees and Tatum was thrown head-first into the windscreen. She landed on the floor of the front passenger seat.

Teagan, who had kept his seatbelt on in the back seat, was unharmed but Tatum lay crumpled on the floor, seriously injured. She was flown by helicopter to the Royal Children's Hospital in Melbourne. Tatum had deep gashes to her forehead, broken glass in her left eye, a ruptured spleen and a bruised kidney, but she was alive. And she had saved the lives of not only her brother and her mother, but also of the motorists who had been travelling down William Street that morning.

COMMUNITY HERO

Karen De Koning had to be cut from the wreckage of the car after an hour of being trapped behind the wheel. The doctors were uncertain about what had triggered her seizure. Karen suffered a broken neck and ankle from the accident and had to wear a neck brace for the next three months. But she was possibly the proudest mum in Australia when Tatum was given multiple awards for her bravery, including the 2011 Ambulance Victoria Community Hero Award.

Paramedics at the scene of the accident couldn't believe such a little girl had shown so much courage and been able to think so quickly when a car was speeding out of control.

When Tatum's grandmother flew out from South Africa to help look after the family, and tried to make a fuss over Tatum, the little girl just smiled.

'Mummy needed my help,' she said. 'I couldn't panic. I just had to be brave.'

Tatum De Koning was a fast thinker and wasted no time in making a decision about what she needed to do to save her family. When it comes to saving lives, time and how you use it can be the most important part of the rescue, and sometimes there is only a split second to make exactly the right decision.

THE FASTEST FIVE SECONDS OF YOUR LIFE

Stephen Jury loosened his tie and shifted from one foot to the other. His mum had yelled at him about making sure he was on time for his first day at a new school, and his new uniform felt tight and sweaty. It was going to be another stinking hot day.

It was the first day of the school year for 1983. Stephen stood on the platform at Boronia railway station, waiting for the next train to the city, along with 200 other people.

Stephen didn't know the man standing a few metres away from him, but he knew what to do when that man suddenly passed out and fell from the platform – smack onto the railway tracks, just as the 8.10 a.m. train to the city came roaring into the station. The train was only 100 metres away and moving at over 60 kilometres an hour. Stephen had five seconds to save a life.

He jumped. 'C'mon mister, please mister,' Stephen muttered as he hooked his hands under the man's arms and tried to yank him up. But it was no good – and the train was hurtling towards them. He rolled the man towards the platform wall and threw himself on top.

The train driver saw the man lying unconscious, the boy in his school uniform leaping down onto the tracks. He slammed on the emergency brakes and blew the train whistle, a long scream blasting into the morning air.

Up on the platform, there was panic and confusion. The stationmaster tried to clear the crowd away, but some people were boarding the train, oblivious to what had happened. Others were running up and down trying to see what had become of the boy and the man. A woman was crying. A baby screamed. The stationmaster and the distressed train driver shouted at people to get out of the way. They uncoupled the rear carriages and slowly moved the front three forward, dreading what they might find.

The stationmaster climbed down to discover Stephen lying on top of the man with his back to the wall. There was only a 30–40 centimetre space between the wheels and the platform, but

Stephen had managed to wedge both himself and the man into it cleanly. Stephen looked up at the stationmaster and smiled.

The man was lifted onto the platform and taken to hospital, where he was treated for cuts and bruises.

Stephen sat on the platform and ran his hand through his hair. His new uniform was rumpled and one of his shoes had been torn off by the train.

'Can I have my shoe back?' he asked. 'I don't want to be late for school. It's my first day, you know.'

The stationmaster found Stephen's missing shoe on the tracks and Stephen caught the next train to school.

STAR OF COURAGE

Later that day, when he phoned his mum, Stephen didn't tell her about the accident. He was worried she'd be cross with him if he confessed to being late for school.

Stephen's mum was anything but cross when, in the same year, he was awarded the Australian Star of Courage and two gold medals from the Royal Humane Society for his heroism.

Usually, grown-ups are the recipients of the Royal Humane Society's gold medal for bravery. It's very unusual for kids to win that award, or the Star of Courage. But the girl in the next story, like Stephen Jury, also won both awards and was decorated in a special service by Queen Elizabeth.

HORROR AND HEROISM

Twelve-year-old Peta-Lynn Mann loved coming home for the school holidays. Her parents ran a safari business at Channel Point on the Timor Sea, 190 kilometres south-west of Darwin where the countryside is wild and ruggedly beautiful. Peta-Lynn loved exploring the bush around her home.

In April 1981, when Peta-Lynn came back to Channel Point for the Easter school holidays, Hilton Graham decided to treat her to a tour. Hilton was like an uncle to Peta-Lynn. He was a business partner of her parents and a good friend to the whole family. He'd even taught Peta-Lynn to drive when she was only eight years old.

On a bright, clear morning, Hilton and Peta-Lynn travelled 20 kilometres south to where her family kept a boat for touring, and the two of them spent a happy afternoon exploring the mangrove swamps. At nightfall, as they were heading back to Hilton's four-wheel-drive truck, their boat accidentally grounded on a sandbank. Hilton climbed out to push it clear. As he jumped into the shallow water, his pistol fell from its holster and he knelt down to search for it in the muddy water. That's when the crocodile attacked.

Hilton barely had time to raise an arm in defence before a snapping bite broke it in two places. He struggled to his feet but the four-metre crocodile lunged again, this time closing its powerful jaws around his right thigh and dragging him into deeper water.

DEATH ROLL

Peta-Lynn watched in horror, but when Hilton cried for help, she fearlessly leaped into the water. Grabbing Hilton's uninjured arm, she dug her heels into the mud and pulled with all her might. The crocodile – not to be so quickly outwitted – went into a death roll, sweeping Peta-Lynn off her feet and dragging both her and Hilton underwater.

They whirled and thrashed in the murky swamp, but Peta-Lynn wouldn't give in and she wouldn't let go. Regaining her footing, she managed to get Hilton's head above water and she dragged both man and crocodile back to the bank. A few steps from the shore, the crocodile let Hilton go – but as he staggered away, it lunged out of the water again, closing its huge jaws around his hips.

For a moment, it looked as if the crocodile was going to win. But Peta-Lynn was stubborn. Wrenching Hilton from the mouth of the croc before it could establish its grip, she dragged the man up the bank.

Peta-Lynn found a safe spot for Hilton 50 metres from the water, and raced back to the truck. With incredible presence of mind, she drove into the swamp, got her injured friend into the truck and drove back to the safari base camp. There was no one there, so Peta-Lynn covered Hilton's wounds with antiseptic powder and wrapped him in a sheet. Next, she radioed ahead, helped Hilton back into the truck, jumped behind the wheel and set off for Darwin, 200 kilometres away.

GOLDEN GIRL

The following year the Queen awarded Peta-Lynn Mann the Royal Humane Society's gold medal for bravery and the Australian Government's Star of Courage.

Though permanently scarred from the attack, Hilton recovered and went on to open a crocodile farm near Darwin.

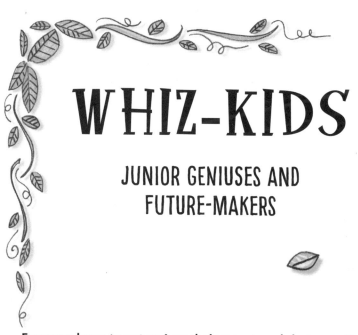

WHIZ-KIDS

JUNIOR GENIUSES AND FUTURE-MAKERS

Everyone loves to get an A on their report cards but sometimes being super-smart can make your life complicated. Being different is never easy and being a genius can set you apart from the rest of the world. Some people love whiz-kids, some people expect too much of them and some people resent their brilliance. Child geniuses have been surprising people for hundreds of years, but every century a new crop of kids come along to amaze adults with what they can do.

BIDDER AT YOUR BIDDING

Ten-year-old George Bidder shifted from one foot to the other as the men from Cambridge University shuffled through their papers and frowned at him. Finally, a bearded professor cleared his throat and looked George in the eye.

'If a flea springs 2 feet 3 inches in every hop, how many hops must it take to go round the world, the circumference being 25 020 miles; and how long would the flea be performing the journey, allowing it to take 60 hops per minute without intermission?' asked the professor, stroking his beard.

George tipped his head to one side and thought for just over a minute – 70 seconds, to be exact. Then he smiled.

'58 713 600 hops, sir,' said George. 'And it would take 1 year, 314 days, 3 hours and 20 minutes.'

IT ALL ADDS UP

George Bidder was born in a small village in Devonshire in 1806. There were a lot of kids in his family and his dad wasn't a rich man, so George wasn't sent to school. Most days he would wander down to the blacksmith's to help in the forge. The blacksmith often gave him odd jobs, and there were always people coming and going.

One day, a farmer who had come into the workshop to have some tools repaired began arguing with the blacksmith about the price. The two men added up the cost of the work but each came up with different answers.

'Excuse me, sir,' said George, 'Neither of you have the right answer. It comes to 2 pounds, 5 shillings and sixpence.'

The men looked at him in surprise and sat down to work out the cost again, only to discover that George was right.

'How did you work that one out, boy? You were very quick with the answer,' said the farmer.

'I like to count,' replied George.

'What's 13 times 17 then, lad?' asked the farmer.

George sorted out the correct answer in a few seconds. The farmer scratched his head and looked at the blacksmith.

'Well, George,' said the blacksmith, 'can you tell us what 130 times 165 comes to?'

'I'm sorry, sir,' said George. 'I don't know what you call a number that's bigger than 999. Is there such a number, and if there is, what do you call it?'

'Why of course there is, lad. That's called a thousand,' answered the blacksmith.

'So 10 times 100 is called a thousand, is it?'

'Yes, that's right.'

'Well, sir, 130 times 165 must be 21 450,' replied George.

The blacksmith and the farmer raised their eyebrows in astonishment. They quizzed George with endless questions and every time the boy answered in an instant.

FORGING TO FAME

George's big brother had taught George how to count to ten when he was six years old and then how to get to 100. George worked the rest out for himself. He used his collection of marbles to help him. He kept them in a little cloth bag in his pocket and he'd squat on the ground outside the cottage and count them over and over again.

As his passion for counting grew, he started to collect dried peas as well. One day, his father saw him kneeling in the dirt making patterns with his marbles and peas and gave him a small bag of gunshot pellets to add to his game. The bag of shot was a fantastic treasure. He could lay it out in sets of five or ten or however he fancied.

Word spread about the boy at the forge, and people began to come to the blacksmith's especially to test his incredible abilities. George became the talk of the county.

Before long, George's dad realised his son was a sensation. He took George on a tour of England and George was billed as 'The Incredible Calculating Boy'. Sometimes they set up a tent, sometimes they staged a demonstration of George's skill in a local hall. People from all across the country paid to hear him answer questions about numbers.

EASY PEASY

In 1816 George was invited to Cambridge University to display his incredible ability to the university's top mathematicians.

After more than an hour of questions, one of them asked, 'Do you remember the first sum I gave you when you arrived?'

'Why yes, sir,' said George. Then he ran the string of figures past the man again.

The professors murmured in astonishment and continued with their questions.

'Divide 468 592 413 563 by 9076.'

It took George less than one minute to come up with the answer. 'It comes to 51 629 838,' said George, 'with a few thousand left over, sir, 'cause it doesn't quite fit.'

George never produced the wrong answer. In the days before calculators and computers people could spend hours calculating sums, but George was like a living calculating machine.

At the age of 11, George still couldn't write his numbers down. As a matter of fact, he couldn't write at all. No one had given him a formal lesson in anything in his whole life. After the Cambridge interview, he was sent to school and at last was taught how to read and write as well as how to write down the numbers that he added up so easily inside his head.

Rich men who were impressed by George's calculating ability offered to pay for his education. At 16, he won a prize from the University of Edinburgh, which meant he could study mathematics and engineering.

George grew up to become a successful engineer. He designed the London telegraphic system and built the Royal Victoria Docks. He never lost his unusual ability to add up figures – even as an old man he could instantly supply the answers to impossible sums. Two days before his death in 1878, a friend was trying to calculate how many vibrations of light the human eye received in one second.

'Put down your pencil – you don't need to work it out,' said old George. 'The answer is 444 433 651 200 000.'

George Bidder wasn't the first or the last 'lightning calculator'. Over the centuries, child prodigies have cropped up regularly to amaze grown-ups with what they know. Zerah Colburn was an American boy, born in Vermont in 1804. He toured America to show what he could do. Eighty years earlier, another small boy called Christian Heinecken could add figures up at a fantastic speed by the time he was three, and he spoke fluently in Latin, German and French. Christian only lived to be four years old

but he was reported as knowing the basics of maths and all the main events in the Bible. But it's fair to say that the most amazing whiz-kid of all time was William James Sidis.

SURPRISE, SURPRISE

'I've got a big surprise for Daddy,' said Billy Sidis, rocking back on his heels and smiling at his mother. Billy was three years old and loved to surprise his parents, especially his dad.

'What sort of surprise, Billy?' asked his mum.

'It's for his birthday. I have a present for him, but I can't tell you what it is. When the people come for dinner, then you'll be surprised too.'

When the guests were sitting comfortably in the living room that evening, Billy slipped into the room lugging a fat book.

'Does anyone know Latin?' he asked.

'Yes, I know a little,' replied one of the guests.

'Here,' said the three-year-old, depositing the book in the lap of the surprised visitor. 'I can read this; I can translate it into English for you. Let me show you.'

The book was called *Caesar's Gallic Wars* and was written in Latin. Proudly Billy read out the first page, then crowed with laughter.

'Oh Daddy, aren't you surprised! I taught myself last week, with a bunch of Mother's old books. All by myself!'

There wasn't much Billy couldn't teach himself. Before he was six he had taught himself Russian, French, German and Hebrew, and later he added Turkish and Armenian to his collection of languages.

APRIL GENIUS'S DAY

William James Sidis was born in New York City on 1 April 1898: April Fool's Day. Billy's mum and dad were both extremely clever people, but Billy was something else, and certainly no fool.

When Billy was six months old his parents gave him a set of alphabet blocks, and by his first birthday he had learned how to spell. When his parents took him for walks in Central Park, kids would come and ask the pretty, fat, blue-eyed baby to count to 100. By the time he was eighteen months old he was reading the *New York Times* as he sat in his highchair in the family apartment. He'd toddle along the bookshelf and pull out any book on request for visitors. Before he was two he read every book he could lay his hands on, and he taught himself to type on his dad's typewriter.

Billy wore his parents down with his endless questions. They bought him an encyclopedia so he could look up his own answers.

Billy's parents took him with them everywhere. With his plump pink cheeks and sandy blond hair, he was often a big hit at dinner parties when he showed off his abilities. One of his favourite party tricks was reciting railroad and bus timetables to astonished grown-ups.

His parents gave him maps, a globe of the world and a calendar, and Billy learned to calculate everything about days. Eventually he would design a perpetual calendar that could show what day of the week a certain date is in any year. Billy also taught himself anatomy, so he could help his dad study for his medical exams.

SHORTCUTS THROUGH THE SCHOOLYARD

When Billy was six, he was sent to school. When his mum went to pick him up on the first day Billy was teaching his teacher a new way to do fractions. It took three days for him to get promoted from the first to the third grade. He graduated from seventh grade six months later.

Too young for high school, Billy stayed at home and decided to write a book. Between the ages of six and eight he wrote at least four books: a textbook on anatomy, one on astronomy and two on grammar. He also started to invent a new language.

By the time he was seven-and-a-half he had passed the Harvard Medical School anatomy exam and the entrance exam for the Massachusetts Institute of Technology. (Harvard and MIT are two of the top universities in America.) He was obviously more than ready for high school – but was high school ready for him?

Billy was eight years old when he started at Brookline High. He barely came up to the elbows of his classmates and he had to stand on a stool to write problems on the blackboard.

The press got wind of the boy prodigy and journalists followed Billy around the school, trying to interview him. Sensational articles about him began to appear in all the newspapers, and soon he was famous as the youngest high school student in America. Not all the articles written about Billy were kind – some journalists made fun of him as a weird freak of nature. A lot of people wanted to believe that there was something wrong with a kid who was so clever.

HELL AT HARVARD

By the time he had spent three months at high school, Billy had completely worn out all his teachers. His dad tried to enrol the nine-year-old at Harvard University, but Harvard refused him – not because he wasn't clever enough; he was just too little. Finally, when Billy was 11, Harvard University decided to take him on as a special student.

Mathematics became his favourite subject and in 1910 he gave a two-hour lecture to the Harvard Mathematical Club. His grasp of mathematics was advanced even for an adult.

When he was 13, Billy was sent to live at Harvard as a boarder. It was a terrible time for him. He was laughed at, teased and harassed. The jealous grown-up students made him the butt of practical jokes, and Billy was constantly humiliated. Young women would pretend they were in love with him and then laugh at him when he blushed and stammered with embarrassment. Young men would trip him up, jostle him in the corridors or make rude remarks when he tried to speak in class. On top of it all, Billy's family was Jewish and there was a lot of anti-Semitism (hatred of Jewish people) at Harvard. His parents organised for him to have his own apartment, but that meant he was lonely and isolated.

Billy went home for the weekends, but the only joy in his week at university was the work itself. He studied Greek, mathematics, American history, astronomy and French. When he finished his first degree, he decided he wanted to become a lawyer; but the situation at Harvard was becoming more difficult for him. Things finally came to a bad end when a gang of bullies caught up with him outside class and threatened to beat him up. Billy had had enough.

THE YOUNG PROFESSOR

Although he was only 17 years old, Billy got himself a job teaching mathematics at Rice University in Texas. He was younger than nearly all his students, which inevitably led to trouble.

Billy was a bit of a slob – he didn't want to cut his hair, he hated having to shave and he dressed sloppily. His own students picked on him for his odd manners, especially his shyness around girls. But the people who often played the meanest jokes on Billy were the press – newspaper articles full of misinformation were published about him and reporters poked fun at everything he said and did. After eight months at Rice University, Billy gave up and went home to Boston to study law.

Billy found his haven in books. Books didn't judge him, didn't care how sloppy he was, didn't mind that he was shy and hadn't worked out how to talk to girls. Books were his only friends.

Billy was a big fan of public transport and spent a lot of time travelling on trams and buses around the city. He believed that people needed to share more, and so he became involved with groups promoting ideas about how to change the world for the better. On May Day in 1919 he was arrested for marching in a parade that was stopped by the police. His parents were furious with him, and Billy had a couple of difficult years trying to break away from their disapproval and start his own life.

THE PRODIGY GROWS UP

Billy was kind and gentle. He was a pacifist; he thought it was wrong to hurt people and he didn't believe in war. He had a small group of friends who appreciated his unusual manners and ideas, but mostly he kept to himself.

When the newspapers tracked him down for comment he said, 'My only plan and purpose for the future is to live near Boston as much as possible and seek happiness in my own way.' And that is exactly what he did.

He collected transit tickets, got himself a job as a clerk, and lived a quiet life.

Experts believe that Billy Sidis's IQ may have been somewhere between 250 and 300 (higher than Einstein's). 'IQ' stands for intelligence quotient – there are tests that you can do to measure it. A regular IQ ranges from 85 to 115. Only about 1 per cent of people in the world have an IQ of 135 or more, though IQ tests can only tell you about one sort of cleverness.

The Sidises didn't bother to help their very clever daughter, Helena, anywhere near as much as they did Billy. In the past, a lot of people thought trying to teach girls academic subjects was a waste of time. They assumed the only thing girls needed to learn about was how to look after the men in their family. Despite this, there have been countless brilliant women thinkers through history, but their stories weren't always recorded.

Over the centuries, women have fought hard to secure better education and there are plenty of astonishingly brainy girls who are turning the tables to prove girls can do anything. Judit Polgar is widely considered the greatest female chess player in world history, and her IQ has been measured at 170 – a score which is even higher than that of the famous scientist Stephen Hawking.

THE AMAZING POLGAR SISTERS

Judit tossed her long red hair to one side and smiled a tiny smile at her opponent. She touched each of her chess pieces and then made her move with ruthless precision. The man opposite sighed. He knew that he had lost the game and that he was going to have to change his opinion about women and chess. Even worse, his opponent wasn't even a woman – just a girl. The kid in front of him was only 15 years old and had recently become the youngest 'grandmaster' in chess history. In over 1000 years of chess playing, there had never been a champion like Judit Polgar.

Judit Polgar was born in Hungary in 1976, the youngest of three sisters. Her dad and mum believed that geniuses are made, not born; they knew their daughters could achieve anything with the right help. They decided to teach the girls at home rather than sending them to school, even though the local authorities were against it.

Zsuzsa (also known as Susan), the eldest, was the first to get interested in chess. Her two little sisters, who were five and seven years younger than Zsuzsa, would sit beside her, fascinated, as she challenged their dad to yet another game. Pretty soon all three girls were hooked on chess.

Lazlo Polgar wasn't an expert chess player – at best he considered himself mediocre. His wife, Klara, didn't play at all. But they could both see that their three girls had a gift for the game, especially Judit. She would spend up to ten hours at the chessboard studying all the possible moves that could be made. After years of practice Judit could calculate the result of any potential move at lightning speed and almost instantly make the right decision.

In 1984, when the Polgar girls were aged 14, nine and seven, the three sisters began attending international tournaments together with at least one of their parents. Zsuzsa quickly became rated as the top woman chess player in the world, but Judit took the spot away from her big sister in 1989 when she was 13 years old. From then on, Judit refused to compete on the women's chess circuit and began to compete exclusively against men.

In 1991, Judit and Susan both attained the position of grandmaster. It was a stunning achievement – at that time fewer than 1 per cent of grandmasters were female. At 15 years and five months of age, Judit became the youngest female grandmaster in history.

In 1993, she caused another sensation when she defeated former world champion Boris Spassky. Many men who had assumed chess was a man's game were forced to think again. One British chess grandmaster described Judit as 'this cute little auburn-haired monster who crushed you'.

At a Rome Open chess tournament, Zsofia, the middle Polgar sister, registered one of the greatest individual performances in chess history. She won eight of nine games and in the ninth, her opponent could only force a draw. In 1997, Zsofia was ranked the sixth top female player in the world. Despite scepticism that women could ever excel at chess, the Polgar sisters continued to astonish the chess world.

THE GAME OF LIFE

For the next two decades, Judit spent several months of each year travelling the world to compete in world-class chess competitions. She considered chess more than a hobby – it was her profession and her passion.

In 2002, Judit beat the reigning world champion, Garry Kasparov, in a game at an international tournament. It was the first time in chess history that a female player had defeated the world's number-one player in competitive play. But in taking on some of the world champions, Judit often had to face criticism. Judit's parents believed that girls could excel at anything and their daughters were living proof of that belief. But despite Judit's many successes, some men refused to play against her because she was a woman. Bobby Fischer, one of the most famous champion chess players of his time, was reported as saying he wouldn't play against her in a professional match because she was Jewish.

Judit remained committed to chess as she grew older, but she also wanted to live a full and rich life. In 2000, she married and later had two children. In 2014, Judit announced her retirement from the chess circuit after 25 years of being ranked among the top players in the world, but she still continues to travel to talk about chess and to advocate for chess in education.

In 2015, Judit Polgar was awarded the Order of Saint

Stephen, the highest recognition that a civilian can receive from the Hungarian government.

CODING THE FUTURE

When people think of tech geniuses, most people think of men like the founder of Microsoft, Bill Gates, or Steve Jobs, who started Apple. But there's a whole new generation of girl innovators growing up in the twenty-first century and they're set to astonish the world with their ingenuity.

SOLVING REAL WORLD PROBLEMS

Lone Pine, Colorado, USA, 2016

'What are you doing with that kit?' asked Gitanjali, as she watched her parents laying out test strips on the kitchen bench.

Nine-year-old Gitanjali Rao was interested in anything and everything to do with science. Both of Gitanjali's parents were engineers, and they shared their love of science and ideas with their kids: Gitanjali and her little brother Anirudh.

'We're testing the water to see if there's any lead in it,' said her mother. 'I just want to be sure that our water is safe to drink.'

'The people in the town of Flint, in Michigan, are having terrible problems with lead in their water,' explained her father.

'I saw that on the news!' said Gitanjali. 'They've announced a state-of-emergency in Flint and now everyone can only drink bottled water because all their water is poisoned with lead. That's really scary.'

'That's why I wanted to check our water, but this test isn't working very well,' complained Gitanjali's mother, studying the test strip and frowning. 'And I paid a lot for the kit.'

'None of those kits work very well,' said Gitanjali's dad. 'You'll have to use more than one strip before you get a reading and then you can't be sure that the reading is accurate. We could take a sample to the local water facility, but it's inconvenient and it takes too long.'

'It doesn't sound very reliable, whatever you do,' said Gitanjali.

Up in her room, Gitanjali started to think about the problem of how to test for lead in water. She simply couldn't accept the fact that there was a city in America where tens of thousands of children were exposed to poison in their water supply. Gitanjali's family were originally from India and she knew that there were problems there too. When she started reading up about the subject, she discovered that cities all around the world are having problems with contaminated drinking water. She felt determined to discover a way to make testing for lead easy for everyone.

Gitanjali loved reading about scientific problems and discovering real world solutions to them. Her hero is the famous scientist Marie Curie, who was the only scientist in history to win two Nobel prizes in two different areas of science. Gitanjali's favourite quote from Marie Curie is: 'We've come a long way but we still have so much more to do when we look ahead.'

Gitanjali looked ahead and puzzled over the challenge of testing for lead in water. She read science websites, books and articles; she started finding out everything she could about testing for heavy metals. Then she started playing around with the problem and looking for solutions.

From reading MIT's website, Gitanjali learned that they had been using nanotechnology to detect poisons in the air. Nanotechnology uses very tiny, invisible things to control atoms and molecules. Everything on Earth is made up of atoms – including lead. Gitanjali started to think about ways she could use nanotechnology to make a tool that would be able to detect lead in water instead of air. She wrote hundreds of emails to scientists working at MIT and other science labs, asking for their advice.

TETHYS, THE GODDESS OF FRESH WATER

When Gitanjali was 11 years old she applied for the 3M Young Scientist Challenge. The competition was for kids with big ideas. Although Gitanjali's parents had been super supportive, Gitanjali was hoping to find a scientist mentor by entering for the prize. Luckily, her brilliant idea meant she was selected as one of the ten finalists in the challenge.

With the help of Dr Kathleen Shafer, Gitanjali started to work on her idea. Gitanjali called her water testing device 'Tethys' after the Greek goddess of water. She had visited Greece with her parents and loved the stories of the ancient gods.

Tethys wasn't the first device Gitanjali had ever made, but it was the most complex. She had already invented a device that detected poison levels in snake bites, which she had named 'Asclepius' after the Greek god of medicine whose symbol is a snake.

Gitanjali's idea was to create a device with a microprocessor inside it. Small, disposable cartridges could be inserted into the device and then dipped into water to test lead levels. The device would connect to a smartphone via Bluetooth and an app, which Gitanjali also invented, using her skills in coding. When the water was tested, the app on the smartphone would show the lead level in the water. Gitanjali's aim was to make the device affordable and easy to use. She believes if everyone could easily test their water regularly, they could prevent their families being harmed by lead poisoning.

In 2017, when Gitanjali was still only 11 years old, she won the US$25 000 ($34 000 in Australian dollars) first prize in the 3M Young Scientist Challenge. She used the money to do further work improving Tethys. The device needs to be perfected before it can be manufactured on a large scale for everyone to use.

Since winning the 3M Challenge, Gitanjali has been awarded more prizes and sponsorship from organisations and companies interested in her invention. Despite all the attention that her prizewinning idea has brought her, Gitanjali is committed to working on her projects and mentoring other kids interested in science. Her experiences developing Tethys have taught her the importance of asking for help, and she's not afraid to reach out to others to seek advice.

Gitanjali doesn't just spend all her time tinkering with her inventions. She also loves to play the piano, bake, swim, dance and fence. Gitanjali has partnered with an organisation, Children's Kindness Network, to spread kindness at the same time as mentoring kids interested in science. She is passionate about helping other girls to enjoy science and has given many talks to groups of girls to encourage them to be brave and ask questions about all the problems that they see in the world around them.

CODING FOR MEMORIES

Emma Yang adored her grandmother. While her parents were at work, Emma's grandmother took care of her and from when Emma was a toddler she would follow her grandmother everywhere. They were so close that the family joked about Emma being 'Grandma's little shadow'.

Emma was seven years old when she started to notice a change in her grandmother. It was only small things to begin with. Her grandmother began to misplace objects and forget plans. Then, one day, in 2012, a friend of Emma's grandmother came to visit the family in their apartment in Hong Kong.

'Emma is so tall!' said the friend. 'How old is she now?'

'She is thirteen years old and so grown-up.'

Emma looked at her grandmother in surprise. 'But Grandma,' she said. 'You know I'm only eight years old, not thirteen!'

Emma began to worry. Her grandmother kept saying odd things, forgetting what day it was and sometimes even forgetting the names of members of her own family. It wasn't long before she was diagnosed with Alzheimer's disease, a brain disorder that damages people's memories. More than 44 million people worldwide suffer from the disease and there is no cure.

When Emma was ten years old, she moved to New York City with her parents. Her grandmother would phone throughout the day, forgetting that she had already called them several times before lunchtime. At family gatherings when Emma and her parents travelled home to Hong Kong, her grandmother would ask the same questions over and over. Then she forgot Emma's birthday – something she'd never done before.

For Emma, one of the saddest problems in her life would eventually pose a question that she simply had to answer. Emma decided she had to do something to help her grandmother, so she asked herself: how could she use her skills in coding to make life easier for people who suffered from Alzheimer's disease?

STARTING FROM SCRATCH

Emma is a talented musician but she also loves to code. Like music, coding is one of her passions. Emma's parents work in technology, and her dad had started to teach her coding when she was six years old. The first coding program she used was called Scratch. Emma quickly went on to learn other coding programs. As much as she loved coding, Emma also loved to read and write and imagine ways that she could use her skills to help people.

In early 2015, when Emma was in Grade Six, she began developing an app called Concussion Checker. The app would be a fast and easy way to assess head injuries. With the help of a mentor, Dr Melissa Leber, and another sixth-grade student, Natalie Essig, Emma drew up a business plan and entered a science competition. When their plan was accepted, Emma flew to San Francisco to take part in Technovation, a giant science fair for girls. Thousands of girls from around the world participate in Technovation every year. They bring their ideas, business plans and app designs with them.

Four hundred teams from 64 different countries competed in the competition. Emma was thrilled when her invention won second place in the world. But the most exciting thing about attending Technovation was the chance for Emma to meet so many girls and women who were also passionate about tech and solving problems in their communities. Up until then, Emma had thought that coding was mostly for boys. It set her thinking about all the amazing things that girls in tech could achieve.

As her grandmother's illness grew worse, 12-year-old Emma began working on a new app that she named Timeless. She wanted to develop an app that could help every Alzheimer's patient. She thought about all the things that technology could do to make it easier for her grandmother to manage daily tasks. Timeless would help Emma's grandmother, and other people who suffer from the disease, to recognise people, see lists of their daily tasks, and help them to connect with their families and friends.

Emma kept working on developing Timeless and found sponsors and mentors to help her perfect it. Her ideas have continued to win prizes and she has become an inspiration to other girls who want to change the world, one app at a time.

FINDING YOUR WAY IN THE WORLD

Tomisin sat quietly in a corner of the classroom, her head down, listening to her computer science teacher, Mr Cole. Twelve-year-old Tomisin Ogunnubi rarely spoke up in class, and no one had noticed how intensely she was listening as Mr Cole explained how to write code to develop smartphone apps.

Like Gitanjali and Emma, Tomisin asked herself a question: how could she use what she'd just learned to create something that could be useful for everyone?

Tomisin lives in Lagos in Nigeria – a city of over 20 million people. The rate of growth in the city has been so intense in the past decade that it has become common for children to get lost in the ever-expanding network of streets. Tomisin decided to work on developing an app that would help children find their way home.

She named her app My Locator and linked it to Google Maps so that it can show both a kid's current location and any location they've saved. It also has an alert button that can send the kid's location to the phone number of someone in their family so that parents can easily find their children if they become lost.

Tomisin is just starting out on her journey to reach more people through her skills in ICT (information and communications technology) but she is already recognised as an inspiration to Nigerian teenagers.

CODE LIKE A GIRL

Gitanjali, Emma and Tomisin may change the future of the world. Each of them intend to keep working on their inventions and hope to make the world a better place through their innovative use of technology. For each of them, meeting other girls who are interested in science has helped them improve their skills.

Code Like a Girl is an Australian organisation that helps bring girls and women scientists together to share their ideas and passion for science. Ally Watson, the founder, started the group in the hope of meeting other women who loved coding as much as she did. Eventually her little group grew into an

Australia-wide organisation that runs events and classes for girls and women interested in learning more about coding – because you don't have to be child genius to learn how to code like a girl.

FERAL KIDS

WILD CHILDREN AND MYSTERIOUS BOYS

When cats, dogs, pigs and other domestic animals go wild, we think of them as feral animals. And sometimes, people who want to give up on civilisation talk about themselves as 'going feral'. But being a feral kid is a lot more complicated than simply living in the wild. Feral kids through history might seem wild and mysterious, almost the opposite of whiz-kids, but even if they didn't know a lot about words and numbers, they understood the world in a different way. They had to use all their senses just to survive. Feral kids have shown that even with all the odds stacked against them, kids can survive in impossible places.

OUT OF THE FOREST

A wild, almost naked boy sat in a tree, watching one of the villagers of Aveyron take firewood into his cottage. The villager's garden had neat rows of root vegetables, and a walnut tree grew beside the stone wall. As soon as the villager was out of sight, the boy ran across the cold, hard ground to the garden and began foraging for potatoes or a walnut or two. It was mid-winter and he was starving. Absorbed in the search, he didn't notice a man approach.

'Wild child!' cried the man, swooping down and grabbing the boy by the arm.

WILD BOY OF AVEYRON

The local commissioner, Constans-Saint-Estève, hurried through the village to the tanner's house. Everyone in the village was talking of the wild boy that the tanner had caught in his garden. As the commissioner of Aveyron, Constans-Saint-Estève decided it was his responsibility to do something about the strange newcomer.

Constans-Saint-Estève tried to get the boy to talk, but the wild child just ignored him and went on staring into the fire, rocking back and forth on his heels. The child was about 12 years old, thin and wiry. Except for the tattered remains of a shirt, he was completely naked. His brown hair hung in a tangled mane down his back. His skin was dirty and covered with sores and scars.

The commissioner eventually managed to coax the boy to come home with him. Early the next morning Constans-Saint-

Estève arranged for local police to take the boy to an orphanage in the town of Saint-Affrique while the authorities decided what to do with him.

The wild boy spent a miserable month in the orphanage. He spat out the soft white bread the staff fed him, and when they dressed him he tore the clothes off his body. He hated the beds, the walls and the way people stared at him. Within weeks every newspaper in Paris was running stories about the 'Savage of Aveyron'. Rumours sprang up that he was hairy and vicious and that he could jump from tree to tree like a squirrel. Meanwhile, the boy lay whimpering in a corner of the orphanage, longing for the forest.

A FRIEND IN NEED

A priest named Bonnaterre expressed an interest in the boy and made a written application to look after him. When Bonnaterre brought the boy back to his village, Rodez, a huge crowd pressed around to stare. In frustration, the wild boy bit anyone who came too close.

Parents who had lost their children came to see if the boy was theirs, but in his five months at Rodez, no one laid claim to him. The priest was busy with other work and it was the gardener of the school, a man called Clair, who cared for the boy.

One day the priest decided to take the boy on a visit to a friend in the country. Now that he was clean, the boy looked anything but wild. He had delicate white skin, a round, agreeable face and long eyelashes. Yet his old habits were strong. He wasn't the least interested in the other guests but found the table laden with food very exciting – he set to work, stuffing as much food into his mouth as he could. When he had eaten his fill, he swept the leftovers into his shirt and went out to bury them in a corner of the garden. The priest realised that educating the wild child was going to be a long and gruelling job.

THE WILDS OF PARIS

The boy grew fat and happy in his time at Rodez. He loved to be tickled and he laughed easily. When the boy had come in from the woods he wasn't housebroken, but Clair managed to persuade him to go outside when he needed to, though the child still had no modesty.

In August, Clair and Bonnaterre took him to the famous Institute for the Deaf and Dumb in Paris, where the boy would supposedly be helped by the best doctors in France. Clair was sorry to part from him and said he would be happy to take the boy back if no one wanted him. They left Paris assuming that he would be well cared for.

But no one came to treat him; no one took responsibility for his care. By November, the boy had lost his sweetness. What manners Clair had taught him were gone. He couldn't bear the endless stream of visitors who came to stare at him. His attendants fastened a leash to his waist to walk him around the grounds for exercise.

The rest of the time he lay in his own filth, refusing to be washed. He grew to hate everyone, biting and scratching anyone who came near him. The famous doctors who had been interested in him at a distance were disgusted by him up close. No one was willing to take on the job of teaching the wild boy how to live with humans.

DR ITARD

There was one young doctor at the Institute who wasn't prepared to give up on the wild boy. Jean-Marc Gaspard Itard was only 25 years old, but he managed to persuade the heads of the Institute to let him try to teach the boy who everyone else thought was unteachable. A nurse, Madame Guérin, was hired to care for the boy's daily needs, and Dr Itard set to work.

One day, Dr Itard noticed that the boy looked up and grunted with pleasure whenever anybody made the sound 'o'. Usually he ignored conversation that went on around him. Itard named him 'Victor' (in French, the 'r' is almost silent) so that every time his name was spoken, the boy would smile.

Itard quickly established that the boy wasn't deaf. In fact, there didn't seem to be anything amiss with him physically. He had a thick scar about five centimetres long on his neck, as if someone had once tried to cut it, but this hadn't affected his ability to make sounds. The problem was that the only thing he was interested in was food. Victor seemed to spend most of his day thinking about the next thing he was going to eat. He stole food and hid it in his room. Many people supposed Victor had lived with wolves, but the boy preferred to eat vegetarian food – nuts and root vegetables were his favourite, preferably raw, but any piece of fruit or dry snack would do.

Dr Itard spent several hours every day trying to teach Victor how to talk, read and write. There seemed no reason why Victor shouldn't learn to speak, but he was not the most willing student. Teacher and pupil would often be at loggerheads, Victor refusing to co-operate and Dr Itard refusing to give up. When the pressure got too much for Victor, he would throw the cardboard letters on the floor and storm out of the room in disgust. But the more Victor resisted, the more determined Dr Itard was that he should continue.

Victor's fits of rage grew more violent. He would bite the mantelpiece and throw things around the room – even burning coals from the fireplace. At the height of his tantrum he would lie on the floor and thrash around until he passed out.

Dr Itard was worried that Victor would injure himself and feared that if the fits continued all their good work would be undone. He decided he had to do something to shock Victor into stopping his tantrums.

One day, he noticed Victor was afraid of heights. The next time Victor started writhing on the floor, Dr Itard grabbed him around the hips, flung the window open and held him half out the window. It was five storeys down to a stone pavement. Victor went limp with terror. When Dr Itard hauled him back inside, Victor quietly returned to his work. Afterwards, he lay on his bed and wept. It was the first time Dr Itard reduced Victor to tears. It wouldn't be the last.

LESSONS END

At the end of five years of intense work, Victor knew only 100 words. He was no closer to being able to read or write, although he could spell *lait* (milk in French). He still preferred to spend most of his time alone. The boy was becoming increasingly unhappy and Dr Itard felt he could do no more. He decided it would be best to leave Victor with his nurse, Madame Guérin.

With Madame Guérin, Victor could at last be himself. She had taught him to drink milk and loved him with a tenderness that asked nothing of him in return. Victor never learned to talk. The only sign that he had once been wild was the excitement he showed at the rising of the full moon, the first snowfalls or the howling of the south wind. The French government paid a pension to Madame Guérin and she cared for Victor to the end of his days. He died in 1828 at the age of 40.

THE QUIET PATH

If a kid like Victor came out of a forest today, doctors would probably say he was on the autism spectrum. For kids with severe autism, being in the world can seem like getting snowed under by an avalanche of information. They have to shut down and go deep into themselves just to survive. Focusing on small things and basic routines can help people on the spectrum find a quiet path in a world that's full of confusion.

Dr Itard didn't succeed in teaching Victor everything he thought Victor should know. His methods were sometimes cruel but the books he wrote about working with Victor helped people learn new ways of educating kids of differing abilities, including autistic kids. In fact, you could say Victor taught Itard more than Itard taught Victor. Through working with Victor, Dr Itard came to understand some very important things about how people learn.

THE GHOSTS OF GODAMURI

West Bengal, India, 1920

'Reverend Singh, please sir. Two *manush-bagha* (man-ghosts) are living in the jungle near here – about seven miles from the village. You must help us get rid of these things. Will you help us kill these ghosts?'

Reverend Singh listened disbelievingly to the villager's story.

'And what does the *manush-bagha* look like?' he asked. 'Have you seen it?'

'It is like a man in its limbs but with a hideous head – like a ghost, a monster! You have guns and drums with you, Reverend Singh. You can save our village.'

'Perhaps we should build a platform in a tree so we can watch the ghost,' suggested Reverend Singh.

Early next morning, Singh and his companions went out to examine the haunt of the ghosts. They found a giant white-ant mound that was nearly as tall as a two-storey building. The ants had left, but it seemed the mound had new occupants. The men erected a platform and kept watch. At dusk, three wolves and two cubs appeared at the opening of one of the holes. Close on the heels of the cubs came the 'ghosts', two scrawny figures with thick matted hair. Some of the men levelled their guns to shoot, but Reverend Singh stopped them. The wolves and ghosts disappeared into the jungle.

'They are not ghosts, my friends,' he said, turning to his companions. 'They are children.'

Singh decided the only way to unravel the mystery was to dig out the ant mound, but none of the villagers would go near the haunted place. A couple of days later, Singh managed to persuade some men from another village who hadn't heard the story of the 'ghosts' to help him.

On Sunday 17 October 1920, the men began breaking up the mound with shovels and the wolves came racing out in terror. Only the mother wolf stayed to fight for her territory. She bared her teeth at the intruders and snarled as they approached her with their upraised spades, but the men killed her with bows and arrows. Once she lay dead, work continued quickly. The ant mound was demolished and there, in the centre in a tangle of hair, fur and flesh, two wolf cubs and the two 'ghosts' lay huddled together.

The men threw sheets over their captives and tied them up. They were rewarded with the wolf cubs, which they would be able to sell at the markets for a good price.

Singh took the children. They were girls. He guessed the big girl was around eight years old and the little one was probably still only a toddler of around 18 months, but it was hard to tell. They were filthy and covered in open sores and scars. Despite being small, they put up a good fight against their captors, scratching and biting anyone who came near them.

Back at the village of Godamuri, Singh built a pen out of poles and placed small bowls of food and water outside the bars. He asked the villagers to take care of the children until he could return with a cart to collect them, and then he went on his way.

Five days later he returned to find the village abandoned. The two small children had been left in the filth of their cage without food or water. They were so weak from dehydration that Reverend Singh had to tear up his handkerchief, dip it in a cup of tea and when it was soaked, put one end into the mouth of each child in turn. The girls shut their eyes and sucked the liquid from the cloth. When they had recovered some of their strength, Reverend Singh loaded them into a bullock cart and spent a week travelling back to his home at Midnapore.

TAMING THE WOLF CHILDREN

Reverend Singh and his wife ran an orphanage for abandoned children, so adding two more didn't seem difficult. A few weeks after their arrival, Mrs Singh gave the girls crewcuts. She also named them – the older one Kamala and the younger girl Amala. The girls spent part of their day in a cage in Reverend Singh's office. He was fascinated by them and believed they had been raised by wolves. He kept diaries about the girls and watched them, trying to work out if he could teach them to behave like human beings.

One thing the girls hadn't learned was how to walk. They moved around on all fours most of the time. They liked searching through piles of rubbish for tasty leftovers and they sniffed everything before they ate it. They avoided the other kids and would sit in a corner of the orphanage and stare at the walls for hours on end. For a long time Mrs Singh couldn't dress them, for the girls would tear the clothes; so she sewed loincloths onto them that they couldn't get out of no matter how they tore at them. At night, the girls slept curled around each other like a pair of puppies.

Although they showed affection for each other, the girls shunned the other children in the orphanage. Benjamin, a toddling baby who tried to befriend them, was bitten and scratched and kept clear of them ever after.

After the wolf girls had been at the orphanage for several months, Reverend Singh decided it was time they had more freedom. They had been spending most of their time in the cage in his office, and when they weren't in the cage they were kept indoors under supervision. In the spring, they were allowed out into the courtyard for a few hours during the day. Someone was always assigned to watch them.

Khiroda was one of the older girls in the orphanage – she'd been found in a bundle of rags on the Singhs' doorstep when she was just a baby. On a sunny Saturday afternoon Khiroda was given the job of watching the wolf girls. They sat in the shade against the wall and watched the other children playing. Khiroda looked up to see the wolf girls heading to the garden gate. One of the smaller children had gone out into the garden and left it open. Khiroda ran after them, but Amala and Kamala were too fast for her – and too fierce. Khiroda ran screaming back into the orphanage, her arms streaming with blood from the scratches and bites the wild girls had inflicted. The alarm raised, all the orphanage staff went racing after them. Amala and Kamala were found lying quietly in the middle of a thicket of lantana bushes and brought back to the orphanage.

Another cage was built for them in the courtyard underneath a jackfruit tree. The Singhs made sure that if they were not in their cage, a grown-up watched them all the time.

KAMALA ALONE

A year after their arrival at the orphanage, both girls fell ill. The Singhs hadn't allowed doctors to see the girls before – they were worried that once word spread about the wolf children in their care, a stream of curious visitors would plague them. They also thought no one would want to marry the girls when they grew up if the truth about their past became known. But now the girls were so sick it looked as if they might die. The Singhs called in a doctor, but it was too late for little Amala. She died within days.

Kamala tried to wake her dead sister. She touched her face, her eyes, her lips. She would not leave the body. Eventually the Singhs carried her away, and for the next six days Kamala sat in a corner alone. For weeks she would go to the places Amala had last been and smell them, looking for the scent of her companion.

As her grief subsided, Kamala became more attached to Mrs Singh. She also befriended the animals that lived in the courtyard and developed a special affection for the baby goats. Slowly, over the years, Kamala became used to life in the orphanage. She began to walk upright and, in a small way, learned to fit in with the humans around her; but progress was slow. After two years in the orphanage, Kamala had learned only two words, and she never acquired enough words to explain where she came from.

As the Singhs had feared, a stream of visitors came to see the so-called wolf child. Kamala, small and wiry in her thin cotton dress with her head shaved, was brought out for the guests to stare at.

Nine years after her arrival at the orphanage, Kamala fell ill and died. She was around 17 years old when she passed away.

LOST CHILDREN

The Singhs thought that Amala and Kamala had been raised by wolves, but people who have studied the lives of wolves find it hard to believe that any wolf would bother to raise human babies. Wolves are usually busy enough looking after their own cubs without having to worry about a scrawny furless human. Like Victor, Amala and Kamala were probably abandoned because they had disabilities that their families didn't know how to manage.

The kid in the next story was neglected and abandoned too, but not in the wild. His story is strange, even for a feral kid; in fact, it's one of the great unsolved puzzles of history.

THE MYSTERIOUS BOY

Nuremberg, Germany, 28 May 1828

It was late afternoon and long shadows stretched across the cobbled street. A boy lurched from one side of the street to the other, leaning on the wall to help support himself. A man was watching him.

'Are you lost, boy?' asked the man.

The boy stared blankly.

'Do you need some directions? I've been watching you this past half-hour and you're walking around in circles. Where are you heading to? Where do you want to go?'

The man used hand gestures to indicate directions because he could see the child was struggling to understand him, although the boy looked to be somewhere between 14 and 16 years of age.

'The tower,' replied the boy.

'The tower? Now what tower would that be, then?'

The boy sighed and swayed unsteadily on his feet. The man noticed he was clutching a letter and asked who it was for. There was no answer, so the man gently took it from the boy. It was addressed to 'The Captain of the Light Horse in Nuremberg, near the New Gate'.

'Ah, it's the New Gate you're after. I can take you there.'

The boy stared at him with sad eyes and said, 'I want to be a rider like my father.'

No one at the captain's house knew what to make of the strange boy. They offered him meat and a mug of beer, but he spat the food out in disgust. When he was offered bread and water, he ate and drank with relief. He could only answer their questions by saying, 'Dunno,' and 'I want to be a rider like my father.'

As the captain was away, the strange boy was shown out to the stable, where he immediately fell asleep in the hay. He seemed exhausted. When the captain returned he was as mystified by the boy as his servants had been. He took the strange visitor to the police station, where the boy answered all questions with the same two replies.

'I want to be such a one as my father was,' he wept

He had two letters in his possession, neither of which did much to explain who he was or how he came to be in Nuremberg. The letters raised more questions than they answered. The police decided to give the weeping boy a name: Kaspar Hauser.

THE CHILD OF NUREMBERG

News of the strange boy being kept at the police station quickly spread through Nuremberg, and all kinds of people came to visit him. They found a teenager, 140 centimetres tall, with soft down on his lips, pale blue eyes and soft curly brown hair. Except for the bewildered expression he so often wore, he had an attractive face. He had arrived in Nuremberg in an odd collection of mismatched clothes: a round felt hat lined with yellow silk and stitched with red leather, a black silk scarf, a grey cloth jacket, a linen vest with red dots, and a pair of riding pants. His toes stuck out through the ends of his boots. In his pocket was a red and white checked handkerchief with a 'K' embroidered on it, and a small envelope with some gold dust inside.

Every visitor tried to engage Kaspar in conversation, but he found company tiring and his expression would quickly become glazed if anyone asked too many questions. He had such a small collection of words that his jailer couldn't help but notice how often he said the word 'horse'. Because of this, one of the policemen had the bright idea of giving him a wooden horse. Kaspar was ecstatic and wept with happiness when he was handed the toy. Soon he had built up a collection of wooden horses that his visitors brought him, and he spent much of his day in jail decorating them and pretending to feed them.

Andreas Hiltel, the jailer at the Nuremberg tower, supplied him with paper and crayons. When Kaspar wasn't tending his horses he drew, until every wall of his cell was covered with pictures from floor to ceiling.

Hiltel brought his children to play with Kaspar. Kaspar

liked 11-year-old Julius immediately but he found two-year-old Margaret scary. She was so small and loud that Kaspar looked alarmed whenever she entered his cell.

'Margaret – she hurt Kaspar?' he asked. Julius laughed and reassured him that Margaret was harmless, even if she was annoying.

The boys struck up a friendship and Julius took it on himself to teach Kaspar how to speak. Unlike Victor and the wolf girls, Kaspar was a fast learner. Every day Julius helped Kaspar expand his vocabulary until Kaspar could communicate with his visitors in a basic way.

'Kaspar many visitors today, Julius,' said Kaspar. 'Kaspar like the lady with the tail.'

'A tail?' asked Julius.

'She come with the man with the mountain,' said Kaspar seriously.

Julius looked at his father and raised his eyebrows.

'I think he's talking about a lady with a long shawl that dragged along the ground,' said Herr Hiltel. 'She came with a big fat fellow – that must be the man with the mountain.'

SO LATE IN THE WORLD

After several months in the jail, Kaspar was moved to the house of a local teacher, Professor Georg Daumer. No one had been able to find out anything more about where Kaspar had come from, and he still couldn't explain it himself.

His fame had spread from Nuremberg to all of Germany. Newspaper articles began to appear about him across Europe.

Though the people of Nuremberg had called him their child, he soon became known as 'the child of Europe'. His sweet nature and innocent manner charmed nearly everyone who met him.

Kaspar could give almost no explanation about where he had come from. It seemed he had been kept in secret isolation for the whole of his childhood. The strange letters he had carried, the packet of gold dust and the peculiar old-fashioned clothes he had been found in added to the mystery. In some ways, he was like a newborn baby – he knew so little about the world.

Professor Daumer set about teaching Kaspar how to read and write. Kaspar learned quickly, and never tired of asking questions. There was much to find out.

'I am already so old and still have to learn what children have already known for so long,' he said. 'Sometimes I wish I had never come out of my cage. I have come into the world so late . . .'

One August night, as he stood at his bedroom window he called out to the professor.

'Who put the candles in the sky, Professor?' he asked. 'I have never seen the night sky before. It is so beautiful.'

Kaspar believed everything in the world had a life and understanding like his own. He found it confusing to have to distinguish between the feelings of animals and people. He often had long and interesting conversations with the professor's cat.

'I have seen your cousin, Herr Cat. Doesn't that interest you?' asked Kaspar as he stroked the cat on the windowsill. 'Your cousin, I'm sure it was your cousin – he looked just like you so he must be your relative. Also, today I saw a dog, very well-behaved,

Herr Cat. He had such nice manners. I am sure if you tried you
could be like him.'

UNRAVELLING THE PAST

Gradually Kaspar became capable of talking about his past, but
it all sounded like a strange dream. As Kaspar often couldn't
distinguish between what he dreamt and reality, it was even
harder to make sense of his story. He said that he had been kept
in a cellar that was only two metres by one metre, with two tiny
windows set in its ceiling. There was nothing in the cellar but
straw, two wooden horses and a wooden dog. For as long as he
could remember, he had lived in this prison. All he could do was
sleep, eat and decorate his toy horses with a collection of red
ribbons. When he woke, a small piece of fresh bread would be
there for him, and some water in a jug.

Towards the end of his time in the cellar, a man had come to
him and tried to teach him how to write his name. For weeks on
end the man tried to teach Kaspar how to pray as well, and when
Kaspar failed to understand he was beaten.

One day, the man lifted Kaspar up and carried him out of
the cellar. Kaspar fainted with the pain of having to stretch his
legs after years spent on his hands and knees. The man spent
several days teaching Kaspar how to walk, but the boy's knees
were permanently damaged from years of inactivity. Every step
was painful. The man promised Kaspar he would have his own
horse if he co-operated.

Eventually the mysterious stranger abandoned him in
Nuremberg with the letters.

THE MAN IN BLACK

Eighteen months after Kaspar arrived in Nuremberg, an incident occurred that showed his past was more tangled and mysterious than anyone had imagined.

Kaspar was in the outside toilet when he saw a man's feet at the door. He was too afraid to move. He sensed that something was wrong. Kaspar had always been afraid of black – black horses and black hens both frightened him. When Kaspar went back into the house, he heard footsteps. The man – clothed completely in black with his face masked by a black handkerchief – was in the hallway.

He lunged at Kaspar with a knife and Kaspar fell to the ground, unconscious. When he came to, he was covered in blood. Terrified that the man would return to finish him off, he staggered into the basement, where he blacked out.

Hours later, Professor Daumer's mother discovered Kaspar in the basement, lying in a pool of blood with a long deep gash across his forehead.

An English lord who had taken an interest in Kaspar's case decided it was no longer safe for Kaspar to stay in Nuremberg. He organised for Kaspar to live with a different teacher 80 kilometres away in the city of Ansbach.

The new teacher, Meyer, was a cruel man who had little sympathy for Kaspar's gentle ways. Kaspar began to feel he was in prison again.

Two years later, a strange man lured Kaspar into the Orangerie in the Ansbach Court Gardens. He told Kaspar he had a message from his mother and promised it would reveal who Kaspar really was. When they were alone, the stranger stabbed Kaspar in the chest with a dagger and left him for dead. Kaspar struggled back to the house of his teacher.

At first Meyer refused to believe Kaspar, and forced him to walk back to the Orangerie to show where the attack had happened. Finally, when Kaspar revealed his wound, he was put to bed, delirious with pain.

'Many cats are the death of the mouse,' said Kaspar. 'Tired, very tired, still have to take a long trip.'

He died three days later on 14 December 1833.

THE LOST PRINCE?

Kaspar was probably no more than 21 years old when he was murdered. Many people believe he was the lost Prince of Baden, who was kidnapped from his cradle because his relatives wanted to inherit his kingdom, but the mystery of Kaspar's origins has never been solved.

In 1924, at the castle of Schloss Pilsach near Nuremberg, workmen who were renovating the building found a tiny dungeon. Inside, among the debris, was a little white wooden horse.

Whoever he was, Kaspar Hauser, the child of Europe, has haunted the imagination of the world ever since he appeared on the streets of Nuremberg.

RULERS

KIDS IN THE CASTLE –
PRINCES OR PUPPETS?

Being your own boss should be the best thing about being a king or queen. But taking the throne early can mean getting pushed around every single day of your life.

TEMUJIN THE IRONSMITH

Chief Yesugei the Brave stepped out of his tent with a small bundle in his arms. The people of the Borjigin and Tayichigud clans emerged from their tents and gathered around him.

'My firstborn – a son,' he announced, holding the bundle out for the tribe to see.

'But what is that in the child's right fist?' cried a woman, as she peered at the red-faced baby.

Yesugei smiled. 'He was born clutching it – a clot of blood the size of a knucklebone,' he said proudly.

The crowd murmured.

'It is a sign,' said the woman. 'A magic omen.'

Yesugei looked down at his infant son. 'Yes, the boy will be a great ruler. I will name him Temujin the Ironsmith. He will rule with an iron hand.'

TEMUJIN'S BRIDE

Yesugei was the leader of the Tayichigud, one of many nomadic tribes that travelled across Mongolia – a huge country in the centre of Asia between Russia and China. The tribe was like a big extended family that moved from place to place with its horses and goats.

When Temujin turned nine, his father decided it was time to find a bride for him. They rode for several days to reach the Onggirat tribe and Temujin was introduced to a shy ten-year-old girl called Borte. Yesugei and the Onggirat chieftains negotiated the marriage and agreed that Temujin should stay for a while to get to know his future bride.

Temujin watched Yesugei mount his horse and ride out of the camp. He would never see his father again.

When Temujin returned home he found the tribe in uproar. On his journey home, Yesugei had met with a tribe of Tatars, traditional enemies of the Tayichigud. They had invited him to eat with them and share their food. Yesugei accepted; but the food was poisoned and he died three days later.

The Tayichigud quickly decided Temujin was too young to lead them. They moved on, abandoning Temujin, his mother Ho'elun and Temujin's four younger brothers and sister.

Ho'elun had no relatives in the tribe and no one wanted to help her raise her children. At only nine years of age, Temujin had to take responsibility for his family.

They lived like wild creatures along the banks of the Onon River. Temujin fished and hunted, while the rest of the family gathered wild fruit, dug roots and tended the few goats left to them. They were often hungry. Temujin grew fierce and wild. In a fit of rage, he killed one of his own brothers in an argument over food.

Four years went by and the Tayichigud heard that Temujin and his family were still alive. They were amazed that Temujin was skilled enough as a hunter to feed his family. They heard that he had killed his own brother. The new leaders of the clan decided he could be dangerous, and they sent men to capture him. When Temujin saw them coming, he mounted his horse and rode into the woods. It took nine days for them to track him down. His captors decided they couldn't afford to take any chances. They put him in wooden stocks, clamping a heavy yoke across his neck and securing his hands, and took him back to their camp as a prisoner. He was 13.

BREAKING AWAY

Over by the campfire, the tribespeople were celebrating.

A huge feast was being served and Temujin's guard kept glancing over at what he was missing out on. Temujin lay on the ground and stared up at the night sky. He was weighed down by the heavy wooden stocks and the back of his neck was raw from where the yoke chafed his skin. As he listened to the laughter from the camp, rage bubbled up inside him.

While the guard looked enviously towards the campfire, Temujin quietly got to his feet. It took all his strength to make his next move. Quickly he swung the stocks at the back of the guard's head. The heavy wood made a dull thud as it knocked the man unconscious.

Temujin squatted down beside the body and glanced towards the campfire. No one had seen.

It took only a few minutes for Temujin to reach the riverbank. He slipped into the icy water, using the wooden stocks to keep himself afloat. Only his upturned face was visible on the surface of the stream.

It didn't take long for a hue and cry to be raised. Temujin closed his eyes and listened to the sound of search parties beating bushes along the riverbank. All night, men with torches moved along the bank and in a wide circle around the camp, searching for him.

When a flaming torch shone brightly into his face, Temujin knew he had been seen; there would be no escape. He looked across the water and met the eyes of his captor. The man nodded and winked before turning away and heading downriver. Temujin couldn't believe his luck.

Just before dawn, the man returned and waded out into the water. He unshackled Temujin from the stocks and helped him to the bank.

'Here's some meat to give you strength,' he said to the shivering boy. 'I am sorry for how the tribe has treated you. Your father was a good chief and you deserved better than this, but you must know that already they fear you.'

'So they should,' said the boy. 'I will not forget your kindness, nor their cruelty. One day, I will take revenge on them and on the Tatars who killed my father.'

'One day, you will be a great ruler. It has been foretold,' said the man.

THE UNIVERSAL RULER

Temujin returned to his family. As he grew older, more families came to join his tribe. When he was 14, he went back to the Onggirat people and claimed Borte as his bride.

By 1206 Temujin was in control of most of Mongolia, and the many tribes that he had drawn together declared him 'Genghis Khan' (Universal Ruler). Two years later, he led his armies over the Great Wall and into China.

In 1215 he captured the walled city of Beijing, the capital of northern China, and from there he moved on to conquer Korea. Temujin was a military genius and a brilliant organiser. Even though his armies were small to begin with, he led successful invasions of great empires. After conquering nearly all of Asia, he headed west to invade northern India, Turkey and Russia until he controlled nearly all the land between the Caspian Sea and the Arctic Ocean. By the time of his death in 1227, the wild boy who had fed his family on fish and roots had become ruler of the largest empire in the history of the world.

HEIR TO THE THRONE

The sun was shining and the fields were thick with wildflowers as young Prince Edward and his entourage left Ludlow Castle. It was 23 April 1483. Beside Edward were the two men he trusted most: his half-brother Sir Richard Grey, and his mother's brother Lord Rivers.

Behind them rode a company of 2000 men. Ten days earlier, Edward had been told of the death of his father, the King. Now he had to travel to London to prepare for his own coronation as Edward V, King of England.

It was a long ride to London and the party would have to detour through Northampton to meet Edward's other uncle, Richard of Gloucester. Gloucester, as the brother of the late king, would act as regent until Edward had learned all he needed to know to govern the country alone. After all, Edward had turned 12 a few months earlier.

Twenty-two kilometres south of Northampton, Lord Rivers set the young king up in an inn for the night and rode back to Northampton with Grey to meet the Duke of Gloucester and discuss Edward's future. At dawn the next day, Lord Rivers and Grey awoke to find themselves locked in their rooms.

GLOUCESTER TAKES OVER

The streets of Northampton were crowded with soldiers and footmen. Edward stood outside the inn with his servants, wondering what could have happened to Lord Rivers and Grey. When he saw his uncle Gloucester riding towards him he felt relieved. Gloucester and his men leaped from their horses and bowed low before the new king.

'I have come to protect you, dear nephew,' said Gloucester. 'Rivers has conspired to have me killed, planning ambushes along the road. Your father wished for me to be your regent, so I must protect you from the treacherous men who surround you.'

'But Uncle,' said the young prince in surprise, 'I have great confidence in my uncle and my half-brother. My mother the Queen has always trusted them and assured me that they advise me well.'

'It is no business of the Queen's to be involved in ruling the kingdom. It is not work for women! As to your servants, they are all traitors,' declared Gloucester. 'Men, arrest them immediately!'

The boy king looked on in horror as all his closest servants and supporters were seized by his uncle's soldiers. Those of the entourage who weren't arrested were ordered to return home. Suddenly, Edward was alone. His uncle appointed a whole new set of servants and guards – none of whom he knew.

'No one but I can protect you,' said Gloucester. 'I am the only one who has your best interests at heart.'

Edward didn't know whether to believe him or not.

SANCTUARY

In London, Edward's mother heard of what had happened and knew her whole family was in danger. She gathered up her younger son, Richard, the nine-year-old Duke of York, and her five daughters, who ranged in age from two to 17. Taking what treasure they could carry, they sought refuge at Westminster Abbey. The church would protect them if no one else would.

On 4 May, the young king rode into London with Gloucester at his side. Only 500 soldiers accompanied them, each one hand-picked by his uncle. Edward wore rich blue velvet, but his face was pale and drawn.

Gloucester and all his men wore black.

'Behold your prince and sovereign lord!' cried Gloucester to the watching crowds.

Some people cheered, but rumours were rippling through the streets. Ahead of the royal entourage were four cartloads of weapons. The weapons displayed had supposedly been taken from Lord Rivers and Grey before they could attack the Duke and seize control of the kingdom, but Edward believed it was all a lie. He had always been a little afraid of his uncle Richard, Duke of Gloucester, and now he knew why.

THE TOWER

'I am sure you will be much more comfortable at the Tower than here in the Bishop's Palace,' said Gloucester. Edward felt a chill creep up his spine.

'I am perfectly happy to stay here, Uncle,' said Edward.

'You may be happy but I do not believe you are safe, my lord. The Tower is much more secure than this place. I can keep a much better eye on you there.'

On 19 May, Edward climbed the long flight of stairs that led to the royal apartments in the White Tower of London. At any other time he would have been delighted to be there, but as he stood at the high windows on the south side and looked across the River Thames, he felt terribly alone. The royal arms glowed in the stained-glass windows, a gold and vermilion design of angels and birds was painted on the walls, and on the floor were tiles decorated with the royal leopards and white harts. It was all very beautiful, but the walls of the tower were three metres thick, and Edward knew there was no escape.

A CRY FOR HELP

Edward was relieved when Lord Hastings came into his apartment with a retinue of servants and a sheaf of papers for him to sign. Hastings had been a loyal supporter of Edward's father and was the only man he felt he could trust. But he was shocked at the unhappy expression on Hastings's face.

'I have news for you, my lord,' said Hastings. 'Today, your Council has appointed Gloucester protector of all the kingdom. There is little sovereign business for you to deal with, for nearly all the royal papers will be handled by Gloucester from now on.'

'What does that mean?' asked Edward, alarmed.

'It means that your uncle is in control of England,' replied Hastings glumly.

'Something must be done to stop him!' cried Edward.

'I will do everything I can to help you, my lord, but your uncle is a powerful man.'

On 13 June, Lord Hastings was accused of treason. He and all members of the Council who were still faithful to the young king were executed. Edward watched from the windows of the Tower as his friend's head was chopped off with a sword.

Edward was due to be crowned in only ten days, but he began to realise the coronation might never happen. Now that Hastings was dead, there was no one he could trust.

THE PRINCES IN THE TOWER

Three days later, Edward was lying on his bed and groaning in pain. He had a bad toothache and his jaw was swollen, but there was no one who could help him. His uncle had dismissed all his servants. The only attendant that he was allowed was an evil-looking man called Will Slaughter, and Edward was loath to ask anything of him.

There was a knock at the door, and Edward sat up and braced himself. When the door opened, and his little brother Richard ran into the room, Edward didn't know whether to laugh with pleasure or cry out in fear.

'Richard! What are you doing here?' he cried.

'Uncle said I was to come to be with you for the coronation,' said Richard, jumping onto the bed beside his big brother.

'But I thought you were in sanctuary with Mother!' said Edward.

'Well, she didn't want me to come at first, but lots of different gentlemen told her she had to let me. I'm so glad to see you! Aren't you glad to see me?'

Edward looked at his brother and felt more afraid than he ever had. Richard was meant to be king if anything happened to Edward. Now both the heirs to the throne were firmly in the power of Richard of Gloucester.

All they could do was wait to see what their fate would be.

Occasionally, Will Slaughter allowed them to play in the Tower gardens, but mostly they kept indoors. The Royal Mint, a small zoo with lions and leopards and the state prison were also at the Tower of London, and there were often visitors milling around in the courtyards.

Sometimes people who came to see the animals would glimpse the pale faces of the princes at the Tower windows.

RICHARD III

On 22 June, when Edward should have been crowned, Gloucester dismissed parliament and postponed the coronation indefinitely. London was full of noblemen who had come from across all England to see the boy king crowned. Richard ensured all of them knew that he thought young Edward was unfit to reign. On 26 June 1483, Richard of Gloucester declared himself to be the rightful king of England, and a few days later he ordered the execution of the imprisoned Lord Rivers and Richard Grey.

A nobleman was sent to tell Edward that his uncle had been crowned king on 5 July.

'Alas, if only my uncle would let me have my life, though I lose my kingdom,' cried Edward.

The princes were never seen alive again. No explanations were offered for their disappearance. Many historians believe Richard of Gloucester was responsible for their deaths. Others claim Richard was innocent and only ever acted in the best interests of his nephews. William Shakespeare wrote a famous play about Richard III that cast him as an unforgettable villain. No one will ever know the exact truth of what happened to the princes in the Tower.

Despite becoming king, Richard was not to reign happily ever after. His only son died before reaching adulthood and he himself died only two years after assuming the throne, at the battle of Bosworth Field in 1485.

Two hundred years later, the turret at the entrance of the chapel of the White Tower was crumbling. The then king, Charles II, ordered it demolished. On 17 July 1674, the skeletons of two children were found in a wooden chest at the base of the chapel staircase. The small bones had fragments of velvet still clinging to them. No one doubted they were the bodies of the princes. Their remains were taken and buried under an altar of black and white marble in Westminster Abbey.

Even though neither of the young princes grew up to rule, their descendants still wound up on the throne of England. Their elder sister, Elizabeth, married the king who overthrew Richard. Sixty years later her grandson, another Edward, became the first and only boy ruler to wear the English crown.

EDWARD VI, BOY KING

Edward VI was only nine years old when he became king in 1547. Even though he had two older half-sisters, Edward inherited the throne. Until recently, girls were always overlooked in preference to boys when it came to inheriting kingdoms.

Everyone was impressed with young Edward. John Knox described him as 'the most godly and virtuous King that has ever been known to have reigned in England'.

His mother had died when he was a tiny baby, but her two

brothers had always taken an interest in their nephew. When Edward's father died as well, the elder uncle, Lord Somerset, became his Protector. But the younger one, Thomas Seymour, had no intention of being left out of the new king's business.

One night in January 1549, as Edward slept peacefully, the small spaniel that lay at the end of his bed leaped to the floor, barking furiously. Edward sat bolt upright as the spaniel rushed to the door that was slowly edging open. There was the loud crack of a pistol shot, and the dog slumped in a heap.

A huge commotion exploded outside his bedroom – men's shouts, a clash of steel and the sound of guards running along the hallway.

Edward jumped out of bed and ran to the door. His favourite pet lay in a pool of blood on the threshold while guards stood either side of his red-faced Uncle Seymour.

'My lord, it was self-defence,' said Seymour. 'I had only come to see how well you were being guarded. I am sorry for having to kill your dog – it did a finer job of guarding you than these soldiers.'

Edward knelt beside his dog and rested one hand on its still-warm body. He didn't want to believe that his uncle wished him harm, but he couldn't help suspecting the worst.

PUPPET RULER

The next day, Edward and his council of advisers ordered Thomas Seymour be arrested and charged with treason. They believed Seymour's plan had been to kidnap young King Edward so he could control the kingdom. Whoever controlled the life of the boy king controlled the whole country.

On 20 March 1549, Thomas Seymour was executed on Tower Hill in London. But that was not the end of plots and schemes designed to turn the young king into a puppet ruler. By October of the same year, Edward's other uncle, the Duke of Somerset, was in prison. Although he was later released, by 1552 he had fallen so far from Edward's favour that he, too, was executed.

The new Lord Protector, the Earl of Warwick, allowed Edward to participate in the ruling of the kingdom a lot more than Somerset had, but at the same time, he made sure his own power increased. Edward made him Duke of Northumberland and granted him more lands and power.

In October of 1553 Edward would be 16 and the government of the realm would be handed over to him completely, but before his fifteenth birthday, Edward developed a hacking cough. He was pale and thin and when he coughed, blood came up with the spit. The Duke of Northumberland was desperate to keep Edward alive – so much of his power depended on the young king's favour. He organised a stream of doctors and herbalists to attend Edward, but rather than curing him, they only seemed to prolong his agony.

On Thursday, 6 July 1553, at six o'clock in the evening, while lightning flashed outside his window and huge hailstones crashed against the panes, Edward whispered his last prayer.

THE NINE-DAY QUEEN

Edward had dreaded the thought of his big sister Mary coming to the throne after him. She was a Roman Catholic but Edward was a Protestant. All across Europe, Protestants and Catholics were killing each other in fights about religion, and Edward was determined that England should have a Protestant ruler. As Edward lay dying, the Duke of Northumberland encouraged him to write a new will ordering that his Protestant cousin, Lady Jane Grey, follow him as queen of England. The Duke had already organised for his own son to marry 15-year-old Lady Jane.

When her father-in-law declared her the new queen, Jane was horrified. Her cousin Edward had been dead for only a few days and she knew she was not the rightful heir to the throne. It belonged first to her cousin Mary, then her cousin Elizabeth.

'The crown is not my right and pleaseth me not,' she said to the Duke. 'The Lady Mary is the rightful heir.'

Her parents, the Duke, her new boy-husband and his mother all argued with her. She must take the crown. Jane fell to her knees and prayed. Finally, against what was in her heart, she stood up wearily and seated herself on the throne.

Nine days later, on 19 July 1553, Jane's father burst into her chamber and ripped down the royal canopy that hung above her supper table.

'You are no longer queen,' he said. 'The Lady Mary and her followers have taken the city.'

'I am very glad of that,' she said calmly.

On 12 February 1554, Lady Jane Grey and her husband,

Guildford, were executed. Guildford wept as they walked in procession to Tower Hill, but Jane held her prayer book tightly and kept her head high.

'Lord, into Thy hands I commend my spirit,' she said in a clear voice as the axe fell.

GLORY WITHOUT POWER

The two Edwards or Queen Jane might have grown up to be great leaders if they'd had the chance, but they got caught up in the adult world of power and politics before they were ready. Just because you're young, doesn't mean you can't have dreams of leading your people. But even those who believe they're born to lead can find life tricky when faced with treacherous adults.

THE CHILDREN'S CRUSADE

Cloyes, France, 25 April 1212 – St Mark's Day
Stephen stretched himself out on the bank of the Loire River and stared up at the afternoon sky. It was late spring and the sheep were scattered across the meadow, quietly grazing.

Stephen spent most of his time out on the hills with his flock, but that morning he had visited the city of Chartres to watch the procession celebrating the day of Black Crosses. Altars were shrouded in black and priests and people went through the streets chanting prayers and carrying black crosses. The priests prayed for Christian Crusaders fighting in the Holy Land. Stephen had heard stories about soldiers from all over Europe who had gone to fight the Mohammedans (Muslims) and drive them out of the land of Israel. Even though he was only a shepherd boy, Stephen longed to join the Crusade, to see the place where Jesus was born and take it for the Christians.

THE MESSENGER

The stranger arrived with the evening light behind him. Stephen saw him from a distance, a small figure clothed in black and bent over as if tired from a long journey. He was obviously a holy pilgrim, perhaps a priest. Stephen shared his supper with the stranger – a crust of bread and a piece of cheese.

'Tell me of the Orient,' said Stephen, as they finished their meal. 'Have you met many heroes on your journey? How goes the Holy War?'

'Not well, my son,' said the man. 'The men of France waver in their faith, the Crusaders are straggling back to Europe and there is no strong leader to take up the banner. The Lord needs a hero to rouse the spirit of the people.'

'I'd give anything to be able to fight for Jesus,' said Stephen.

'I'm glad to hear you say that, Stephen, because I have come to you to reveal your mission,' continued the man. 'Here is a letter for you to take to the King of France. It will command him to furnish you with all you need. I want you to lead the Fifth Crusade – the last Crusade – that will reclaim the Holy Land once and for all time. You are the chosen one who will lead the children of Europe to conquer the infidels. You will not need weapons. Your faith alone will conquer the unbelievers. You will go to the infidels with love in your heart and they will convert to the true faith and become Christians. Because you are pure of heart, you will succeed where all others have failed.'

For a moment, Stephen couldn't speak. He knelt before the man and bowed his head.

'May I be worthy of this honour,' he said.

RAISING THE BANNER

The next morning, Stephen woke on his straw pallet in his parents' cottage and looked around him in astonishment. He knew his whole life was about to change.

Stephen told his parents he could no longer tend the sheep because he had a mission from the Lord, but they didn't believe him.

'Don't you realise that the priest must have been Jesus Christ! How can you argue with the commands of Christ?' he cried, angrily waving his letter at them.

For the next month, he told his story to everyone in and around the village of Cloyes. It was very frustrating – people shouted him down and some even laughed at him. At the end of May, he slammed the door to the cottage and took the road to the city of Saint-Denis. He carried nothing with him but his crook and a little wallet that his mother had made for him in which he kept the precious letter. He was determined to take his message to more God-loving people than the peasants of Cloyes.

Saint-Denis housed a famous shrine that thousands of pilgrims came to visit. Stephen headed straight to the steps of the shrine and told the people who gathered around him of his meeting with the man he believed was Jesus Christ. He told them he had a mission to save the Holy Land and that every God-loving child in Europe would find glory by joining him. He was a passionate speaker.

Pilgrims abandoned the shrine and came to listen. Children, especially, were enthralled. Stephen told them that it was children alone who would win the war of the Holy Land. The grown-ups had failed and the kids would show them how.

THE GREAT MARCH

Word began to ripple across France from village to village until every child had heard of the boy at Saint-Denis who would lead them to glory in the Holy Land. In streets and fields, everyone was talking of the boy and his letter to the King.

'God can wait no longer,' shouted Stephen to the crowds who came to see him every day. 'We can wait no longer. We will show you knights and warriors what children can do!'

Thousands of children took up the cry. They marched across France to meet with Stephen, carrying candles and with crosses held aloft. Parents shouted and wailed to see them go, but the children believed they were acting under a higher law than their parents – their orders were from God.

Rich and poor, boys and girls left their homes and took to the roads. Many had lost their own fathers in the wars for the Cross. Some adults joined in, because they loved the idea of pure young children rescuing the Holy Land. A motley crew of thieves and tricksters also followed, considering children easy prey.

King Philip Augustus of France never saw Stephen's letter, but he heard of the crusade. He was torn about what to do. He thought the idea was crazy, but if he told the children to stop the Pope might be angry. What if the crusade really was ordered by God?

After consulting with his advisers, he issued an edict that the children should return home. He would not support them in their crusade. But still the crowds of children swelled and went on marching to the city of Vendôme to meet with Stephen.

The children were unstoppable. If their parents locked them up, they broke down the doors and rushed to join the processions. They sang and shouted and waved banners. Many parents believed the devil was at work.

Meanwhile, the rumour of the new crusade had spread to Germany. A boy called Nicholas, from a town near the city of Cologne, took charge of the German crusade.

Like Stephen, Nicholas was a 12-year-old shepherd. He told of seeing a cross of blazing light in the sky and hearing a voice that told him the light was a promise of his success in the holy war. Many German parents hoped that their kids would lose heart by the time they reached Cologne, but by June 1212 Nicholas had an army of 20 000 children marching up the snowy Alps out of Germany to Italy.

Back in France, thousands of children – most of them no more than 12 years old – were marching across the blazing summer countryside. The kids were hot, thirsty and starving. Stephen reassured them by saying the heat was God's way of drying up the sea so that they could walk to the Holy Land when they reached the coast. But God's plan seemed confused, because the smaller children began to die of dehydration. The road to

Marseilles grew littered with their corpses. Fights began to flare between the children.

When the young crusaders asked Stephen how much longer it would be, he would always reply, 'Soon.' But secretly he was worried. Luckily, the peasants of the countryside were generous and fed the procession as it passed through their villages, but Stephen had no idea how far it was to the coast.

It took a full month to reach the sea. The children had travelled over 500 kilometres on foot with few supplies, and many had given up or been captured by their parents or thieves. Thousands had died. Thirty thousand children had left Vendôme, but only 20 000 stood on the hill above Marseilles. They sang as they marched into the city, where they were welcomed by the citizens.

A WAY THROUGH THE WAVES

In the early morning, Stephen went down to the shore and knelt before the sea. He prayed that God would part the waves as he had for Moses and that a path would open up and allow them to walk all the way to the Holy Land. The blue sea lay calm before him. Little white waves broke on the beach and birds wheeled overhead. Day after day Stephen prayed, but the waters wouldn't part for him and the children became restless. Some left Marseilles and returned home.

When Stephen was at his lowest, he met two merchants who traded with the east, Hugo Ferreus and William Porcus. They offered to help.

'For the cause of God and at no cost, we will supply ships to take you,' announced the traders.

Stephen was ecstatic. This was the way through the sea that God had meant. It was the miracle he had prayed for.

'All other Crusaders and pilgrims have to pay to go to the Holy Land,' he preached to his followers, 'but we will go for nothing. This is a sign that God is with us.'

But many of the children were afraid of the sea. They had expected to walk to Jerusalem. When the final tally was made of those brave enough to cross the sea, only 5000 children and adults had volunteered to continue the crusade.

On the morning of their departure, the churches of Marseilles were full to overcrowding with children and the people who supported their quest. Stephen led the assembly down to the docks and his young army boarded the ships, singing praise to God. Everyone else ran to the cliffs and watched the seven ships and their white sails disappear over the horizon.

THE LAST OF THE CRUSADES

It was eighteen years before the fate of the child crusaders was known. In 1230, an old priest returned from the Holy Land. He was one of the adults who had accompanied the 5000 in 1212. He told the people of France how two ships had been smashed to pieces in a storm off the coast of Sardinia and all hands lost less than a week after setting out from Marseilles. The other five ships sailed on to Algiers, only to discover that it would have been better if they had gone down too. Porcus and Ferreus were not just merchants – they were slave traders. When the first ship docked, the children were delivered straight into the hands of African slavers. Some of the remaining ships sailed on to Alexandria, in

Egypt, where many of the children were bought by the governor to work on his lands. The priests were sold to a sultan, who took them to his palace in Cairo. They were much luckier than the children, as they were given work as teachers for the sultan and his family.

Hundreds of the children were taken on even further, to Baghdad, and most of them accepted that they would be slaves for the rest of their lives. Eighteen were murdered for refusing to convert to the Muslim faith.

Although Porcus and Ferreus were not punished for their crime towards the children, they were hung for trying to organise a plot to kidnap a German king.

The German children, led by Nicholas, had no more success than the French. They trudged over 1000 kilometres of cold, rugged terrain to reach the city of Genoa in Italy. Only 7000 out of 20 000 survived the journey.

At Genoa, the sea was no more willing to part for Nicholas than it had been for Stephen. Thousands turned back. A small group straggled on to Rome and approached Pope Innocent, who told them they had been deceived but asked them to sign a vow to fight in the Crusades when they grew up. In 1217 he launched another Crusade and the children who had hoped to win the Holy War with love were forced to take up arms.

It was not until 1291 that the Crusades finally petered out and the Europeans left the people of Palestine alone.

DANCING TO THE PIPER'S TUNE

Because the Children's Crusade ended so badly, a lot of people wanted to forget about it. History likes to remember the winners. One way the story of the kid crusaders was kept alive was as the fairytale, 'The Pied Piper of Hamelin'. For the parents whose kids left Germany never to return, Nicholas of Cologne was a real Pied Piper. But not all kids' crusades wind up as fairytales. Sometimes those who lead with faith and kindness can change the world.

THE DALAI LAMA

Lhamo sat in the sweet-smelling straw and flapped his little arms. His mother had sent him to the hen-house to collect eggs, but he had climbed into the nesting box and sat down, clucking like a hen and laughing. His big brother, Samten, found him there.

'Come back to the house, Lhamo. There are visitors arriving at the gate. Stop acting like a chicken!'

Lhamo laughed again and climbed out of the chicken coop. He was two years old. Though Samten was nearly five, it was Lhamo who led the way in the race back down to the house.

The year was 1937 and Samten and Lhamo lived in the village of Taktser in the north-east of Tibet. The village lay on a plateau and was surrounded by fields of wheat and barley. Bright turquoise tiles edged the flat roof of Lhamo's home, and in the middle was a small courtyard. Prayer flags fluttered on top of a tall pole in the courtyard, for Lhamo's family were devout Buddhists.

THE ROSARY BEADS

Lhamo was sitting by the fire in the kitchen when the visitors were shown into the room and invited to sit down. Lhamo didn't wait for an invitation to climb into the lap of the stranger who wore a long soft cloak lined with lambskin. He touched the string of rosary beads that the man wore around his neck.

'I have this? Mine?' asked Lhamo.

'I will give it to you if you can guess who I am,' said the stranger.

'You Sera-aga,' replied Lhamo.

The stranger looked across at his companion. 'And who is this man?'

'Amdo Kasang,' said Lhamo. The stranger nodded.

'And the master who is talking with your parents. Who is he?'

'He Losang,' said the small boy impatiently. 'I have the beads now?'

The three strangers stayed the night with Lhamo's family and in the morning when they were setting out to leave, Lhamo came running from his bed.

'I want to go too. I go with Sera-aga,' he shouted.

His mother laughed and scooped him up into her arms, apologising to the visitors as she ushered them out the door.

After the visitors had left, Lhamo's parents discussed who the holy men might have been. They knew that a lama (head monk) had recently died at the nearby monastery of Kumbum. Buddhists believe that the spirit of a person is reincarnated after death – the old spirit of a wise person will come back in the body of a new baby – so a lama can be replaced by a child. Perhaps the visitors had been searching for the new lama for Kumbum.

Lhamo's parents were partly right. Sera-aga and his companions were searching for a new lama; but not for Kumbum. They were looking for a new Dalai Lama, ruler of all Tibet. The 13th Dalai Lama had died two years earlier in 1933. At his death a great search began for the boy who would be his incarnation.

Tibet is a very religious country with an ancient culture. Since 1391, the country had been ruled by a succession of Dalai Lamas. Tibetans believe that the Dalai Lama is so holy that he is reborn or 'reincarnated' over and over again. For centuries, each new Dalai Lama had been found in his boyhood by a group of lamas who were sent to search for him. They followed strict rules about how to discover where the spirit of their new ruler could be found, for they had to be sure they had found the right child.

THE TEST

A few days later, a huge search party of senior lamas came back to Lhamo's house. Lhamo's parents were amazed to think their cheeky two-year-old son could be the reincarnation of the Dalai Lama. They ushered the group of holy men into their small home. The lamas believed that if Lhamo really was the reincarnation of the Dalai Lama he would have retained some memories of his past life. The fact that he had been able to name the men who had visited a few days earlier was a sign that he could be the boy for whom they had been searching.

The lamas and other officials set out a number of objects on a flat table for Lhamo to examine. The tiny boy walked confidently into the room. He was no higher than the knees of most of the visitors. They all watched him as he looked at the strange things laid before him.

The first thing they offered him were two identical black rosaries. Lhamo quickly picked the one that had belonged to the 13th Dalai Lama. Next, they presented him with two identical yellow ones. Again, he instantly laid his tiny hand on the one that had belonged to the previous Dalai Lama.

Two small drums were put before him and the boy looked at them carefully. One was a simple drum of the type that monks beat during prayers; the second was much more ornate, with golden straps. Lhamo looked at each of them and picked the simple one. Again, he had made the right choice.

Lastly, they presented him with two walking sticks. For the first time he seemed hesitant. He touched one, and then the other, before choosing the correct walking stick – the one that had belonged to the 13th Dalai Lama. Later, the monks discovered the second walking stick had also been used by the Dalai Lama, but he had given it to a friend who had in turn given it to the lama who was testing Lhamo.

The monks and officials were convinced. This boy was surely the reincarnation of the 13th Dalai Lama. The monks who had been assigned to search for the boy believed that many other small signs had been revealed to them. With Lhamo's parents' permission, the child and his brother Samten were taken to the nearby monastery of Kumbum.

THE YOUNG TRAVELLER

Lhamo was lonely at the monastery. He was too little to have lessons, and Samten was taken away by tutors for hours on end to learn to read and write. Lhamo would play on his own – often the same game of making up parcels and then setting off on his hobby-horse on a long imaginary journey. Perhaps he understood what his future would be even though he was so small.

A week after Lhamo's fourth birthday, a party of over fifty people set out on foot and horseback to take him to the city of Lhasa so he could live in the Dalai Lama's palace. It would be a three-month journey.

ENTHRONEMENT

As the party approached Lhasa, Lhamo took off his peasant clothes, put on the robes of a monk, and climbed into a gilded palanquin in which he would be carried to the palace. The roadsides were crowded with people dressed in their best clothes. Horns, flutes, drums and cymbals sounded, and people sang and danced as the new Dalai Lama passed by. Lhamo looked out the sides of his palanquin with amazement. The entire population of Lhasa had come to see him arrive. The air was filled with the scent of incense and wildflowers.

As Lhamo entered the throne room, everyone rose to their feet. The Chief Abbot took his hand and led the small boy towards the Lion Throne. It was made of gilded wood with two carved lions at each corner. Five square cushions, each a different colour and covered with brocade, made the throne over two metres high. When Lhamo was seated on his throne, the ceremony began.

Throughout the long and complicated ceremony, which included performances, dances, prayers and blessings, the new Dalai Lama was quiet and paid attention to all his duties. He blessed his teachers and the members of his government, drank sweet herbs from a golden cup, and was presented with a golden wheel and a white conch shell – symbols of his spiritual and earthly powers. The peasant boy was now the 14th Dalai Lama of Tibet.

That day, 22 February 1940, four-year-old Lhamo Dhondrub was renamed Jetsun Jamphel Ngawang Lobsang Yeshe Tenzin Gyatso – Holy Lord, Gentle Glory, Compassionate One, Defender of the Faith, Ocean of Wisdom. Tibetans would refer to him as Yeshe Norbu, the Wish-fulfilling Gem, or simply as Kundun – The Presence. The kings, government officials and maharajas who came to Lhasa to see him enthroned would know him as His Holiness, the Dalai Lama, leader of the people of Tibet.

FREEDOM IN EXILE

The 14th Dalai Lama's reign was never going to be easy. Tibet had been isolated from the rest of the world for centuries but in the twentieth century there had been continuing invasions from China.

After his enthronement, the Dalai Lama spent his childhood studying the history and religion of his country. On 17 November 1950, he assumed full political power. He was only 15 years old but the people needed his leadership. Eighty thousand Chinese soldiers had invaded and the people of Tibet were suffering. Their lands were being handed over to Chinese farmers and Tibetans

were living in terrible conditions. They continued to resist
Chinese rule but the invading army crushed all demonstrations.

In 1954, the Dalai Lama went to Beijing to try to make peace
with the Chinese, but without success. The situation got worse,
not better, and on 10 March 1959 the biggest demonstration in
Tibetan history was held in Lhasa. Thousands of people marched
through the streets. The Chinese army put a brutal stop to the
protests and the Dalai Lama was forced to flee his country. He
had argued for a peaceful resolution to the conflict and for
freedom and independence for his people, but now his life was
at risk and he needed to fight from a safe haven. Thousands of
Tibetans followed him into India, where he set up a 'government-
in-exile' in Dharamshala. By 2009, nearly 150 000 Tibetans had
left Tibet to be with the Dalai Lama.

In exile, the Dalai Lama has continued to fight for the rights
of his people from his new home in India. He has travelled the
world, drawing attention to the plight of Tibet and seeking
support from other countries for a peaceful resolution to his
country's problems with China.

'With truth, courage and determination as our weapons,
Tibet will be liberated,' he said. 'Our struggle must remain non-
violent and free of hatred.'

In 1989, the Dalai Lama was awarded the Nobel Prize for
Peace.

Over the many decades that the Dalai Lama has lived in India,
he worked to democratise the Tibetan government. In 2011 he
signed a document to hand over the leadership of Tibet to the
elected leader of Tibet's government-in-exile. It marked the end

of 368 years of the tradition of Dalai Lamas being the political leaders of Tibet.

In the sixty-plus years that the Dalai Lama has been in exile, China and the world have changed. The Dalai Lama became convinced that a middle-way approach could be best for both China and Tibet. He has proposed that Tibet might remain within the People's Republic of China but the Tibetan people should have self-rule and control their own destiny.

As the Dalai Lama grows older, discussions have been held as to whether there will be a 15th Dalai Lama to follow on his work, but the current Dalai Lama believes, in the spirit of democracy, that this will be for the Tibetan people to decide.

REBELS

FIGHTING BACK AGAINST THE SYSTEM

Rebels might seem the opposite of rulers, but when people fight for a better way of doing things, they can inspire millions of people to think differently about what's important. Being a rebel is about saying 'no' to injustice and rebels can be the inspiration for a better world.

It takes a special kind of strength and courage to swim against the tide – to say 'no' when the world tells you something that you know in your heart is wrong – especially when you have to stand up to people bigger and more powerful than you.

THE KID FROM THE COORONG

The strangers arrived at Bonney Reserve in a big, shiny black car and got out clutching brown-paper parcels. Ruby watched them from a safe distance.

'They reckon they're gonna take us to the circus,' said her brother, as he stood beside her.

'The circus?'

'Yeah, what do you reckon?'

'I reckon I want to know what they've got wrapped up in all that paper,' said Ruby.

The Hunter kids lived with their grandmother and their relatives in the South Australian Riverland region. They were Ngarrindjeri people and spoke their own language as well as English. For thousands of generations, the Ngarrindjeri people had belonged to the Riverland where the Murray River meets the sea – the Coorong.

Ruby had been born on the banks of a billabong and she loved to climb the big gum trees by the water's edge. She and her three brothers and big sister spent their days playing in the bush around their home.

THE BLACK SHOES

The kids watched as the strangers opened the brown-paper parcels for them and took out a new set of clothes for each of the children.

Ruby slipped on a pair of lacy white socks and buckled up the black shoes that the stranger handed to her. She couldn't believe how shiny the shoes were. When she stared down at them she could almost see her own reflection in the patent leather. But something about the whole situation bothered her.

Ruby looked up at her grandmother. 'I don't want to go to no circus, Nani. I want to climb a tree and hide.'

'You got to go to the circus, Ruby,' said her grandmother.

'We're going to have a lot of fun together,' said the lady who had given Ruby the clothes. 'You can have jelly and ice-cream and there'll be laughing clowns. I'm sure you'll enjoy it, Ruby.'

Ruby looked up and nodded politely but she couldn't help feeling there was something wrong about what was happening. Suddenly, she felt too hot in the new clothes. She wanted to take off her new dress and the red coat with its fur collar and run back into the bush – but then a policeman arrived and he and the strangers herded all the Hunter kids towards the big black van.

Someone pushed Ruby into the van. Ruby was confused. If they were going to a circus, why was there a policeman there? Why were there bars on the windows of the van? She looked across at her grandmother, standing beside the van, and saw a look of pain in her eyes. Ruby felt an answering stab of fear.

As the van sped away from the camp, Ruby and her brothers and sister looked out through the window. Ruby pressed her face against the bars and her eyes stung with tears. Their grandmother had one hand against the side of her face and the other held out – was she waving or reaching out? The car turned a corner, and Ruby's grandmother and the camp disappeared from view.

DRIVING INTO DARKNESS

It started to grow dark and the Hunter kids had run out of talk. They sat silently in the back of the van, each thinking their own thoughts. Ruby lay down and put her head on her sister's lap, and the rhythm of the long journey lulled her to sleep.

Hours later, Ruby woke up. She was alone. A bright light was glaring down on her.

'How'd they get that little sun in here?' she thought. She discovered she was lying on a narrow bed in a small room. The 'little sun' was a single light bulb in the ceiling. Ruby had never been in a room with electric lighting before – she was used to sunlight, firelight and starlight.

She shuddered, even though the room wasn't cold. She sat on the edge of the bed, staring down at the hazy reflection of her face that she could see in her black patent leather shoes. She was eight years old and she had never felt so alone in her life.

FIGHTING BACK

Ruby never saw her grandmother again. Nani's grief was so great at being separated from all her grandkids that she died of a broken heart before Ruby had finished growing up. Each of the Hunter children were sent to different foster homes or institutions, and it was many years before they had a chance to see each other again. In one afternoon, the authorities had smashed Ruby's family to pieces.

Ruby wound up in a children's home too. There was no one to kiss or cuddle her any more. She had to do everything she was told, and do it quickly, or she was punished. But she never forgot her past. She didn't know where she belonged any more, but she knew she had to hang on to her memories.

At 13, Ruby ran away from the children's home and took to living on the streets of Adelaide. The years that followed were long and hard and often filled with a sort of hopeless despair.

Sometimes the weight of remembering was almost too much; but she kept fighting and refusing to let go.

She was still a teenager when she met the man who would later become her husband, Archie Roach. Archie's story was like Ruby's – he'd been stolen from his parents and forced to live with strangers.

Ruby grew up, and she and Archie had two boys of their own. But because Ruby had missed out as a kid, she was determined to be a mother to as many children as she could. She was a foster mother to as many as 12 kids at once. She also worked as a counsellor and with homeless kids.

Ruby spoke out to let people know about the bad things that have happened to her people. Both Ruby and Archie became well-known singers and songwriters. In 1994, Ruby became the first Australian Indigenous singer to sign with a major record label. She released two albums and won many awards for her music and her performances.

THE STOLEN GENERATIONS

The Hunter kids weren't the only Aboriginal kids who were treated this way. No one knows exactly how many children were stolen from their parents, but the number is probably somewhere around 100 000. Nearly every Aboriginal family in Australia has been affected by the cruel government policies that tore children from their homes.

For most of the twentieth century, right through into the 1970s, the Australian government tried to make Aboriginal kids forget their black heritage. Officials believed that if the kids were taken away from their families they would become more like white people. But the stolen children refused to forget.

On 26 May 1997, a 700-page report was presented to the Australian Parliament. The report was called *'Bringing them home'* and it told the stories of thousands of children who had been taken from their families. It was the first step in the battle to gain acknowledgement of the wrong that was done to the Aboriginal people.

The kids who had said no and refused to forget who they were began to turn the tide. On 26 May 1998, exactly one year after the *Bringing them home* report was tabled in parliament, the first 'Sorry Day' commemorations were held. 'Sorry Day' became a day to remember past wrongs and to think about how to build a better future for all Australians.

HOPE, LOVE AND AN APOLOGY

In 2004, Ruby and Archie worked with an orchestra to create a musical about Ruby's life. The musical was simply called 'Ruby' and it told her story from the Coorong to being stolen from her family and then eventually finding hope and love.

Ruby's deep, rich voice often moved her audiences so much that they would break down in tears. Many of Ruby's and Archie's songs told stories of the pain and suffering of First Nations Australians. Together they toured the country, sharing their music with audiences in big cities and small, remote communities. Their songs helped people understand just how important it is to remember the true history of the Indigenous people of Australia.

It wasn't until 13 February 2008 that the then prime minister of Australia, Kevin Rudd, made a formal apology to the thousands of Aboriginal and Torres Strait Islander children who were the stolen generations.

On the day of the announcement, Ruby and Archie watched the apology on the big screen at Federation Square in Melbourne. Archie wept and Ruby comforted him. Later in the day, they performed together at a free concert. Archie sang a famous song he had written, 'Took the Children Away', and Ruby sang back-up. It was an anthem for all the stolen generations.

Sadly, Ruby died of a heart attack on 17 February 2010, almost two years to the day after the government's apology. She was only 54 years old, but in those 54 years she had triumphed over pain and heartbreak and inspired thousands of people with her love, her music and her courage.

The fight for reconciliation is not over yet, but those who have followed Ruby's example continue to say 'no' to forgetting, and keep fighting for respect and justice.

DEMAND THE IMPOSSIBLE

During the 1960s millions of teenagers around the world organised protests against the way grown-ups were failing them. In France, a huge movement sprang up in May 1968. School and university students joined with unions and organised a national strike that brought the country to a standstill. Their slogans were 'Be realistic, demand the impossible', and 'It is forbidden to forbid'.

Every generation needs to have kids who are brave enough to stand up for what they believe is right. In March 2018, high school students from Orlando, Florida, in the USA, led a nationwide protest against America's gun laws and hundreds of thousands of children walked out of their schools. Children around the world have staged strikes to make their governments take action against climate change. No one should ever underestimate the power of children.

Though not every campaign succeeds, sometimes when children shout 'no' to injustice they can change the world.

One group of kids in Africa in the 1970s refused to accept the way things were and they made everyone stop and listen. Their story is frightening – getting yourself heard can be dangerous – but these kids hung in there and kept at it. They shouted so long and so loud that their cry is still being heard around the world today.

SOWETO UPRISING

South Africa, 16 June 1976

One cold smoggy morning the kids of Soweto woke up full of excitement. They dressed for school as usual, but over 10 000 of them had no intention of going to classes. All over the township, they poured into the streets and began moving towards Orlando. Some were clutching posters they had made. In their black and white uniforms they were marching to protest – to take on what the grown-ups couldn't.

Hector Pieterson was 12 years old and he was really wound

up. Things were going to change and he was going to help. He buttoned up his school shirt and joined his big sister, Antoinette, in the street outside their tiny house.

A shiver of expectation was rippling through Soweto. 'Soweto' is an acronym for 'South Western Townships'. In 1976 it was South Africa's biggest city with a population of two million people. It was also South Africa's biggest ghetto. Only black South Africans lived there, and under the oppressive system of apartheid they were denied all sorts of basic human rights. Black people weren't allowed to use any of the facilities white people used; they were not even allowed to sit on the same seats in the parks. Black people were not allowed to own land, nor were they allowed to travel without having special 'passes'. Even though more than 75 per cent of the population was black, they were not allowed to be involved in any political groups. People who spoke out against the system were often beaten, imprisoned and murdered.

Nearby in the 'white' city of Johannesburg, 1.5 million people lived in an area five times the size of Soweto.

A third of the households in Johannesburg had swimming pools, but the black families of Soweto didn't even have running water or electricity in their homes. Black people were only allowed to live in Johannesburg as servants to white people. As far as the whites were concerned, Soweto existed simply to provide cheap workers for the white city.

The children of Soweto were angry – and with good reason. On top of all the other difficulties that black students had to contend with, the government was trying to force the students to be taught in the Afrikaans language. Only 8 per cent of the population of South Africa – all white people – spoke Afrikaans. It would be of little use to black kids, who already spoke their own African language as well as English. Afrikaans made it extra difficult for them to learn, and thousands of bright kids began to fail the impossible exams they were set. It was another blow to the self-esteem of the black people; another way of keeping them poor and powerless. The kids were not only determined to protest, they were going to fly the black flag of resistance for everyone to see.

Hector and Antoinette quickly met up with kids from their school. The streets were packed with students – thousands of them. They waved placards that read 'Away with Afrikaans' and 'To Hell with Afrikaans'. Some of the girls danced. Antoinette and Hector joined in the singing and chanting. By nine in the morning the chants of 'Power! Power!' were echoing all over the township.

THE DAY THAT NEVER ENDED

The students converged on Vilakazi Street on the border of Soweto. They had only a vague idea of what they would do once they were there. They just knew they wanted to be heard; to let the world know what was happening. The student leaders hoped to make speeches and decide as a group what their next step would be. They never got the chance.

Police officers had spotted crowds of children moving towards each other and radioed to Johannesburg for tear gas and reinforcements. Three hundred heavily armed policemen were waiting in Vilakazi Street. One policeman threw a stone at the students and the kids retaliated by throwing stones back. Within minutes, the police opened fire.

Everyone was dumbfounded. They didn't even run. No one had thought they would be shot for simply protesting. For a terrifying moment, they stood in the middle of the road while bullets rained down on them.

Hector fell in the first round of fire. Antoinette was beside him in a moment, screaming for someone to help them. An older student, Mbuyiselo Makhubu, swept the dying boy into his arms and ran, his shirt growing stained with Hector's blood. Antoinette ran beside him, crying out in pain and horror, as they searched for somewhere to shelter Hector. There was smoke and tear gas everywhere.

Students ran in every direction. Some threw more stones at the police in retaliation and the bullets kept flying.

Mbuyiselo laid Hector's body gently in the back of a nearby car. Hector had died in his arms. Antoinette knelt beside her only brother and wept.

Hector Pieterson was one of the first children to die in the Soweto student protests. Within 48 hours of his death, 65 black people died as they fought back against the brutal police attacks. During the months of unrest that followed, 300 people were killed and over 11 000 injured.

There is a saying in South Africa that when Soweto sneezes, the whole country catches cold. The kids had triggered a sneeze that would make the whole country shake for years to come. Despite the deaths, the kids kept fighting. They were going to make things happen, and not even bullets would stop them. No political parties or grown-ups could claim credit for the protests that followed. Press statements were issued by teenagers, and the black youth movement became one of the most powerful forces in South Africa.

NEVER FORGET

The sixteenth of June 1976 is often talked of as the day that never ended. It is a day that belonged to children who helped bring down and transform one of the most racially oppressive governments in the world.

All through the 1980s, the rebellion continued. No matter how they were punished, the people wouldn't be silenced. In 1994, Nelson Mandela, the black political leader who had spent 27 years in prison because he opposed apartheid, was elected President of South Africa. It was the first universal election (where everyone was allowed to vote) that the country had ever held. The long struggle to dismantle apartheid was bringing freedom and South Africa was finally a democracy.

The anniversary of Hector's death is a national holiday in South Africa. It's officially named 'National Youth Day' to celebrate the courage of young people who fight to make the world a better place. It's also a day of mourning.

On National Youth Day, people visit the Hector Pieterson Memorial which was erected on Khumalo Street in Soweto, not far from where Hector was shot. The memorial was built in the 1990s to honour all the young people who died in the struggle for freedom and democracy. On 16 June 2002, the Hector Pieterson

Museum opened next to the memorial so everyone can learn the story of the children and their fight.

Hector Pieterson was buried in the Avalon Cemetery. His gravestone reads:

ZOLILE HECTOR PIETERSON
AUGUST 19 1963 – JUNE 16 1976
DEEPLY MOURNED BY HIS PARENTS, SISTERS
AND A NATION THAT REMEMBERS
TIME IS ON THE SIDE OF THE OPPRESSED TODAY
TRUTH IS ON THE SIDE OF THE OPPRESSED TODAY
ONE NATION
ONE PEOPLE

CHILD BRIDE, GIRL REBEL

Payal walked along the edge of the sugar cane fields that lay outside her village. A small girl with stringy black hair sat next to a cage on the far side of the sugar cane. For Payal, the girl sitting next to the cage symbolised everything she feared for her future and the future of the girls of her village.

Payal Jagid was born in 2000 in Hinsala, a small village in Rajasthan in the north of India. When she reached her tenth birthday, she began to dread the fact that very soon her parents would arrange her marriage. Most girls in her village were married between the ages of ten and 13, and there was no reason why Payal's parents would make an exception for her. Millions of young teenage girls around the world are married every year.

International aid organisations estimate that 39 000 teenage girls marry every day. Payal didn't want to be one of them.

But then, in 2012, just when her parents began to discuss who Payal should marry, Mr Kailash Satyarthi arrived in the village of Hinsala.

Kailash Satyarthi is a world-famous activist for child rights. For decades, he has fought to improve the lives of children around the world by campaigning to end child labour. He also formed an organisation called Bachpan Bachao Andolan to work on protecting children across India from exploitation and cruelty.

Satyarthi had come to the Payal's village because it had been chosen to be a Bal Mitra Gram (BMG), or 'child-friendly village'. Satyarthi pioneered the idea of child-friendly villages where children are free from any type of exploitation. In a BMG, every child must be enrolled in school and children are encouraged to become involved in helping guide the community by forming a children's council to advise the local government.

PAYAL'S POWER

Payal was amazed by what she learned about her rights. To discover that she had the right to say no and the right to receive an education made her think twice about her parents' desire for her to marry young. She began to protest against child marriage and insisted on her right to continue studying at school.

Payal also began to realise that there was another age-old tradition in the village that was making the lives of girls and women difficult. In Payal's village, every Hindu married woman was required to wear a veil and keep her face covered at all times.

The practice is called *ghunghat prat* and is not uncommon in northern states of India. When the days are long and hot, the veil can be stifling. The tradition also meant that few women engaged in conversations about the future of the village, as communicating through a veil can be difficult. Payal hated the way it stopped women from being involved in discussions about her community.

Payal became so argumentative about the issue that she was elected as the head of the Bal Panchayat – the children's council – in her village. Thanks to her work, 46 children were admitted to local schools. The children began to know their rights, and the women of the village, once they removed their veils, began to be involved in making decisions for the benefit of the whole community. Along with her two sisters and her brother, Payal has become an active voice in the life of her village.

FROM HINSALA TO THE WORLD

Not long after Payal began participating in her village's children's council, she was invited to Delhi, along with Kailash Satyarthi, to meet the then American president, Barack Obama, and his wife, Michelle. Photographs of Michelle Obama hugging Payal made millions of people around the world aware of Payal's work.

In 2013, when Payal was 13, a delegation from Sweden selected her to be a jury member of the International Children's Peace Prize. Payal flew to Sweden to join the jury of children who would select the winner of the prize.

Payal and the jury selected Malala Yousafzai, the Pakistani girl who fought for the right of girls to be educated. In 2014

Malala would go on to win the Nobel Peace Prize jointly with Payal's mentor, Kailash Satyarthi.

Payal's dream is to become a teacher so that, through education, generations of girls and boys can be lifted out of poverty. Knowing her rights gave Payal the strength to say 'no' to traditions that she knew in her heart were wrong. Following your heart can be the first step in changing history.

SUPERSTARS

FAME, FORTUNE AND HITTING THE BIG TIME

Plenty of kids dream about being famous. But being famous doesn't mean you'll change history. Fame also doesn't always bring happiness or riches. Lots of people are famous for fifteen minutes, but unless they do or make something that touches people's hearts or changes their lives, their fame doesn't last. The kids in this chapter used their talents to change the way people thought about what it means to be famous.

THE KID WHO KNEW WHAT HE WANTED

Three-year-old Yehudi leaned forward in his seat and tilted his blond head to one side, listening intently. He always sat quietly between his parents when they visited the theatre to hear the San Francisco Symphony Orchestra perform. That night, a famous violinist named Louis Persinger played a beautiful solo.

It was a regular Saturday event for the Menuhin family, and Yehudi loved it – sitting high up in the darkened gallery. He closed his eyes and imagined he was flying with the music.

Afterwards, Yehudi asked the same question he asked after every concert.

'Could I have a violin, please Mama, please Papa?'

'One day, Yehudi,' replied his mother.

Yehudi's parents were having trouble finding enough money to pay the rent and, besides, Yehudi was so tiny. There was plenty of time, if only the small boy would be patient. But Yehudi couldn't wait.

THE TIN FIDDLE

All of the Menuhins' friends and relations heard about Yehudi's plea. For his fourth birthday, a friend of the family went to Macy's – a huge department store – and bought Yehudi a smart toy violin. It was made from tin and was just the right size for a four-year-old. Yehudi would be able to pretend he was a great concert violinist, just like Louis Persinger.

Yehudi could hardly contain his excitement as he peeled back the wrapping paper of his birthday present and saw what lay inside; the longed-for violin. He lifted it from the box and laughed with pleasure. At last! The grown-ups all smiled as he tucked the instrument beneath his chin and closed his eyes to concentrate. He raised the toy bow and drew it across the strings, to produce a rough squeaky noise.

Yehudi's face distorted with rage. He threw the tin violin and the bow on the ground and sobbed.

'It doesn't sing!' he shouted. 'I hate it! I want a real violin! I want a violin that sings!'

A few months later, when Yehudi's grandmother heard the story about the birthday present, she sent some money to cover the cost of a proper, small-sized wooden violin for her grandson. It took some time to persuade Louis Persinger to take Yehudi on as his pupil. Yehudi was taught by someone else to begin with, but once Persinger heard the boy play, he knew there was something special about him.

PRACTISING PERFECTION

Yehudi Menuhin was born in New York City on 22 April 1916. His family moved to California in 1918.

By the time Yehudi was seven, he was ready for his first public performance. Persinger accompanied him on the piano at a recital by the San Francisco Orchestra. The boy caused a sensation, and word of his incredible ability began to spread across America.

It was obvious to Yehudi's parents that he was a different kind of kid. They sent him to school for one day before deciding he was better off learning at home with his two little sisters, Hephzibah and Yaltah. His mother taught the children to read and write, and Yehudi happily spent three hours a day practising his violin.

As Yehudi's reputation spread, people invited him to travel to Europe and study under some of the most famous musicians in the world.

When he was ten years old, Yehudi was invited to perform at Carnegie Hall with the New York Symphony Orchestra. Only the best performers in the world got to play at Carnegie Hall, and orchestra members couldn't believe the chubby blond kid would be up to it. The conductor suggested to Yehudi that he should play a simple piece by Mozart, but Yehudi insisted on doing a difficult Beethoven concerto.

In rehearsals, Yehudi had to ask the conductor to tune his violin because the pegs were too hard for him to turn. The other musicians grew even more suspicious. They all grumbled to themselves. How could this little squirt possibly lead the whole orchestra in such a difficult piece of music? The concert would be a disaster.

TRIUMPH AND TOURS

On 27 November 1927, Yehudi stepped out onto the stage at Carnegie Hall and into history. The audience and the orchestra were astounded by his beautiful performance, and plans were set in motion for his first nationwide tour.

Yehudi owned two quite reasonable violins, but he had to borrow a top-quality instrument for his concerts. When one of his rich fans heard that Yehudi performed on borrowed instruments, he invited the Menuhins to visit him.

'You must choose any violin you want,' announced the millionaire. 'No matter what the price. Choose it; it's yours.'

Yehudi picked a violin with a sweet and mellow sound. It was named 'Prince Khevenhüller' and had been made by the famous Italian violin-maker Stradivarius in the eighteenth century. Stradivarius violins are worth millions of dollars each.

Yehudi was so successful that his father decided to give up his job as a teacher so he could manage Yehudi's career. Together they toured America and the world for several months of each year. By the time he was 17, Yehudi had performed all over Europe, America and Australia. He made recordings and commissioned new music from composers. Many pieces were written especially for him.

When Yehudi grew up, he married twice and had four kids, one of whom became a pianist. As well as continuing to play violin, Yehudi began to conduct orchestras. His energy and interest in everything around him made him one of the most sought-after musicians of the twentieth century. He performed to audiences in every corner of the world from South America to India. He learned to play jazz and Indian music, wrote books and became involved in countless organisations that fight for peace and human rights. He even took up yoga; he believed that headstands helped his playing.

In 1963 he opened a music school in London, and in 1965 Queen Elizabeth made him a knight, and then later a British lord. He finally took his title – Lord Menuhin of Stoke d'Abernon – in 1985, when he became a British citizen. Right up to the very end of his life, Yehudi toured the world, conducting concerts and sharing the joy he found in music. He died on 12 March 1999, aged 82, while visiting Berlin, and he was mourned by millions. The three-year-old who had begged for his own violin had become a legend in his own lifetime.

THE KALGOORLIE KID

Eileen stood in front of the shop window and pressed her face against the glass until a small foggy cloud appeared.

'What is that, Mum?' she asked, staring at the huge, dark, shiny instrument in the music-shop window.

'Surely you know it's a piano, Eileen.'

'It looks so grand – it must make a big sound. How does it work?'

'You see those white things and the little black ones – they're the keys and you push them down to make the music.'

'It must be so much nicer than a mouth organ. I'd do anything to have one.'

'One day I'll show you how it works. One day when Daddy's struck gold and we're rich we'll have one, and then you can play all you like, my darling.'

It was 1919 and Eileen Joyce and her mum were in Melbourne on their way to the West Australian goldfields. Eileen was seven years old and until then, she and her mother had lived in Zeehan, Tasmania, in a little hut at the foot of a mountain.

After years in the west searching for gold, Eileen's dad had written to tell them he had enough to pay their fares.

From Melbourne, they took a steamship to Adelaide and a wagon across the Nullarbor Plain. Eileen made herself a mattress from straw and sacking and slept by the campfire on the long journey west to Kununoppin, a tent city on the edge of the goldfields.

THE PUB PIANO

Life was tough for the Joyces and in two years her father's lucky seam had petered out. The family had to move on again. In 1921 they settled in Kalgoorlie and Eileen's father took up work in someone else's mine. Her mother took in laundry and Eileen was sent to a Catholic convent school. The richer girls at the school were taught piano by one of the nuns and Eileen longed to have lessons too, but they cost sixpence each and the Joyces never had a penny to spare.

One day her mother took Eileen down to the local pub. At the back of the bar room stood a battered and beer-stained upright piano. It was out of tune and some of the keys didn't work at all, but Eileen's mum taught her how to play the popular tunes that they both knew and every afternoon, Eileen would slip into the cool dark pub and tinkle the keys.

Eileen grew fiercely determined to earn enough money to pay for her lessons. She took to busking in the streets of Kalgoorlie. After school, she would walk to the edge of town where the miners were returning from work and play her mouth organ. She made sure her father never caught her, and she kept her pennies in a tin in the little lean-to that she slept in at the back of the family bungalow. When a neighbouring boy stole her hard-won savings, she punched his lights out. She was going to have piano lessons and nothing was going to stop her.

BIRTHDAY PRESENT

At the beginning of the new term, Eileen approached the nun who taught piano and held out her sixpence.

Eileen was the fastest-learning pupil that the convent had ever seen. Word spread of her ability and a generous stranger paid for her lessons to continue.

On the night of her tenth birthday, Eileen climbed the steps to the pub and hurried into the bar room for a quick practice session before going home for her birthday tea. To her horror, there was an empty space where the piano had been.

Eileen walked home in a state of misery. She tried to look enthusiastic about the party tea that her mother spread out on the kitchen table.

'By the way, Eileen,' said her mother, 'there's a little something for you in your room.'

Eileen opened the door to her bedroom and stared. Her uncle and father laughed at her expression as they stood on either side of the pub piano. When Eileen lifted the lid and touched the keys she found the piano had been tuned and all the damaged keys repaired. She threw her arms around her father and hugged him tight.

PERTH AND PERCY

Everyone in Kalgoorlie came to know of the extraordinary kid at the convent school who could play the piano like a virtuoso. The local priest wrote to the top Catholic school in Perth, Loreto Convent, and asked them to take Eileen as a scholarship student.

So at 12 years of age, Eileen kissed her parents goodbye and headed off to boarding school and a whole new world of possibilities. Not long after she arrived at the school the famous composer, Percy Grainger, and an international pianist, Wilhelm Backhaus, came to visit Loreto. Friends had told them of the young prodigy, and they wanted to see her for themselves. They were so impressed that they wrote letters to the newspaper asking the people of Perth to help Eileen study in America or Europe.

Back in Kalgoorlie, the miners got together to help pay Eileen's expenses. None of them had forgotten the fiery kid who had stood busking on street corners, and everyone wanted to help. When a couple of rich Perth businessmen offered to chip in as well, the public fund to help Eileen Joyce was up and running.

LEIPZIG, LONDON AND THE WORLD

In September 1927, before her fifteenth birthday, Eileen enrolled at the Leipzig Conservatorium of Music, where gifted performers from all over the world came to study under some of the best teachers in Europe. By the time she was 18, she was being invited to perform as a soloist with some of the world's top philharmonic orchestras. The miners of Kalgoorlie followed her successes in the newspapers as she went on to perform for the BBC and record the soundtracks for British movies. Eileen came home to tour Australia twice during the 1930s. During World War II, she toured the bombed cities and towns of Europe with the London Philharmonic Orchestra in an effort to raise people's spirits, even though her own husband had been killed in wartime action with the Royal Navy.

In 1950, a film was made of Eileen's life, which documented her journey from the goldfields of Western Australia to the concert halls of Europe. Eileen spent most of her life touring the world, from South Africa to the Soviet Union – she became

Australia's most travelled musician of her time. Her career as a concert pianist continued until 1962, when she retired from public performing. She died in March 1991 at the age of 83.

HOLLYWOOD HEROINE

At the same time as little Yehudi Menuhin was wowing world audiences with his violin playing, and Eileen Joyce was busking to earn money for piano lessons, a chubby-cheeked three-year-old named Shirley Temple started dance lessons at Mrs Meglin's Dance Studio in Los Angeles, California.

Shirley spent two years hoofing around with a bunch of other pre-school kids before she was officially 'discovered'. One day in 1932, a pair of movie-makers turned up at the dance studio looking for kids to star in a series of short films they were making. Shirley didn't like the look of them. She hid under the piano and cringed when one of the men pointed to her and said, 'We want that one.'

THE BLACK BOX

Shirley Temple made six short films for the Educational Film Corporation, but the only thing educational about them was what Shirley learned about hard work.

'This isn't playtime, kids,' said the director on the first day of filming. 'It's work.'

One other little girl and a whole tribe of boys performed alongside Shirley. The films were called 'Baby Burlesks' and featured a bunch of very small kids pretending to be grown-ups.

Shirley discovered acting could be pretty dangerous. She was tied to a stake and pelted with clods of mud, knocked flat in a wrestle with a boy, and seated in a cart which was tied to a frantic ostrich that zigzagged across the sound stage before colliding with a wall, throwing Shirley from the cart.

The children's mothers weren't allowed onto the set, and any kids that misbehaved were punished by being put inside a black box, with a block of ice inside it. Shirley had to either stand, lie down in the puddle or sit on the ice block in total darkness. After two sessions in the black box, Shirley paid close attention to what was asked of her.

By the end of 1933, five-year-old Shirley had made eight Baby Burlesks, appeared in five comedy shorts, had six 'walk-on' parts and one bit part in a bigger movie.

Then Shirley was cast as the lead in a movie called *Little Miss Marker*. It made her a star. There were a lot of child stars before her and there have been many since, but none that have made as big an impact on the world.

MUD PIES, MUD PIES

Shirley Jane Temple was born on 23 April 1928. She had dimples, a mane of curly blond hair and loads of spunk. In many ways she was just an ordinary kid who wanted to do ordinary kid things; but even simple things can get complicated when you're a superstar.

Shirley had a bodyguard to protect her from kidnapping, and he had to follow her everywhere she went. Her home was surrounded by a two-metre chain link fence. A photo-electric eye guarded her bedroom window, and every other window in the house was fitted with electric circuit sensors connected to the local police headquarters. Despite all the security, Shirley could still find ways to get into trouble.

The Temple family lived in Hollywood, and all day every day, busloads of tourists stopped outside to gawk at the home of the biggest movie star of 1934: Shirley Temple. A tour driver would recite everything he knew about Shirley and her family. Sometimes Shirley would watch and listen, squatting in the bushes behind the fence.

Even though she generated millions of dollars for the movie studio that she worked for, she got very little pocket money of her own, and like any kid, she was always scheming to increase her piggybank savings. One day, as she sat in the bushes watching the tourists get off the morning bus, she had a brainwave.

Building work was being done on her house and Shirley struck a deal with the builders. Next morning, when the first tourist bus arrived, she was ready, standing outside the gate. Her bodyguard stood beside her, watching with a disapproving frown. In front of her was a neat row of mud pies lined up along the pavement. She'd made a little sign that they were for sale: small ones five cents, large ones 25 cents. They sold out instantly. The bus drivers were enthusiastic and Shirley was kept busy squashing more goop into her mother's pie tins.

After a while, Shirley's bodyguard became uneasy about the crowds of strangers and reported Shirley's antics to her mother. Mrs Temple quickly came running down to the gate.

'No more mud pies,' she said disapprovingly.

'They aren't mud,' Shirley replied. 'They're cement.'

Mud or no mud, Shirley was given a lecture about talking to strangers and marched back up to the house, but not before she'd pocketed her earnings.

MILLION-DOLLAR BABY

Shirley never tired of performing. She had a huge amount of energy and could outstrip most adults, especially when it came to dancing for hours on end.

There was no time for school. Shirley had her own private tutor, who gave her lessons in between film takes in her own private bungalow on the movie lot.

Celebrities from all around the world came to visit her. Everyone wanted to know her, including all the other famous movie stars in Hollywood as well as presidents and princes. By the time she was six, Shirley was one of the most famous faces in the world. Millions of dolls were made in her image; every little girl wanted a Shirley Temple doll of their own.

For her eighth birthday in 1936, Shirley was sent over 135 000 presents from all around the world, including a pair of wallabies from Australia. Of course Shirley couldn't keep so much stuff, and most of it was given to charity. Her parents did let her keep the white model racing car with red leather seats that had its own lawnmower engine, but when Shirley bumped into someone on her first spin around the studio grounds, the car was relegated to the garage at home.

GETTING DOWN TO BUSINESS

Between the ages of six and 14, Shirley starred in 24 films. She cheered up America and a world caught in poverty and depression, and her films earned enough money to rescue the movie company Twentieth Century Fox from big debt. She made millions of dollars for the people who were connected with her career.

You'd think that Shirley would have been rich, but through a combination of bad luck and bad management there was very little left of her fortune by the time she was a grown-up. Shirley gave up acting when she was in her twenties, and after having three kids, she grew interested in politics instead.

THE DARK SIDE OF STARDOM

Not all kid superstars have been half as lucky (or half as famous) as Shirley Temple. Performing is really hard work and not every child loves it as much as she did. Most child stars have a pretty rough time.

Shirley Temple and Yehudi Menuhin were both lucky to have very protective parents who managed to shield them from the downside of being a star. But plenty of kids wind up being forced to work really long days and get caught up in a world of grown-up problems, from drug addiction to bankruptcy. There are hundreds of child stars whose adult lives are nothing but a downhill slide into misery. Many of them have ended up suing their parents for the money that they worked so hard to earn. Some, like Macaulay Culkin of the 'Home Alone' movies, even resort to 'divorcing' one or both of their parents in the course of court battles about money and control.

Child stars can generate millions of dollars of income in a very short period of time, but often their fame is short-lived and they're quickly forgotten. If you really want to be remembered, setting world sporting records may be a better place to start.

SHANE GOULD, GOLDEN GIRL

Shane looked up. There they were again; those signs. 'All that glitters is not Gould.' A grinning American waved the sign as he stood in the stands overlooking the Munich Olympic pool. Shane nodded shyly and walked on by.

Shane felt excited and confident as she prepared herself for the 400-metre freestyle. She knew she was ready for this race and she knew she could win it. Swimming was Shane's life. Ever since she was nine years old and had won her first silver medal at the New South Wales Swimming Championship, she'd been working towards Olympic gold.

When the starting gun went off, Shane cut the water like a knife. She knew she was swimming well; she felt light and smooth. The water rushed past beneath her. All her movements were precise, her arm strokes exact and powerful. The other competitors didn't have a chance. She took the lead and held it for the entire race.

When Shane climbed out of the pool and mounted the podium to receive her gold medal she became the youngest Australian Olympic medallist in history. She was 15 years old.

WATER BABY

Shane Elizabeth Gould was born in Sydney on 23 November 1956. She loved the water from babyhood. When bathtime was over, she cried to get back in the water. Before she was three she could swim underwater at the pool with her eyes open, and at five she was snorkelling around the reefs of Fiji. By the time she was 15, she held every women's world freestyle record from 100m to 1500m.

Shane had the perfect physique for a swimmer; she was tall and slim with wide shoulders and narrow hips. By the time she was 13 she knew that her gift for swimming was something special. She gave up all other interests and gave herself over to competitive swimming. She set her alarm for early-morning training, watched her diet and kept a logbook of her training routines. Her persistence and single-mindedness paid off. Between April 1971 and January 1972, she set seven new world records. By July of 1972, she was so confident that she'd win gold at the Games that she asked her parents if she could have her braces removed just for the competition. She knew the cameras would be flashing and she wanted to look her best.

Fifteen-year-old Shane Gould won three gold, one silver and a bronze medal at the 1972 Olympics. Every gold medal represented a new world record time in that event.

Shane became the only swimmer in history to hold all freestyle world records (100m, 200m, 400m, 800m, 1500m and the 200m Individual Medley) at the same time. She was also the first swimmer to win five medals during the same Olympics. In the same year she was voted both ABC Sportsman of the Year and Australian of the Year.

WHEN THE RACE IS OVER

Australia and the swimming world were shocked when Shane decided to retire from competitive swimming in 1973. Her coach tried to change her mind, but Shane's mum and dad had always told her to give up swimming if it stopped being fun. Shane had achieved more than many athletes achieve in a lifetime and she was tired of being in the spotlight. Three years later, at 19, she married and moved to a farm in Western Australia to start a family. Her new passions became her four children, the environment, and becoming involved in her local community.

In 1981, Shane was awarded an MBE (member of the Order of the British Empire). 'I deserve it more for being a mother than for winning races,' she said to the press.

As her children began to grow up, Shane went to work as a sports coach, counselling other sportspeople. Eventually, she returned to swimming to coach other swimmers and to compete in 'Masters' competitions for older swimmers.

In 1999, Shane published a bestselling autobiography, *Tumble Turns*. She has written many articles and other books about sport. She returned to study and completed two Masters degrees – one in Environmental Management and another in Contemporary Art.

Shane is also a successful businesswoman and a dedicated photographer. In addition, she has volunteered her time to serve on many boards of charitable organisations. Winning can make you a star, but real winners learn that life is bigger than any single competition.

OUT OF THE DUST

Phiona stood by the door on the dusty verandah and watched shyly as the other slum children gathered around chessboards. Phiona thought the chess pieces were beautiful and the children looked so happy. Their faces were bright with excitement as they picked up the chess pieces and placed them on the boards. More than anything, Phiona wanted to feel that happiness too.

Phiona Mutesi lived in Katwe, a vast slum on the edge of Kampala in Uganda. Her home was a tiny, dusty shack that she shared with her mother and brothers. She had no shoes, no education and few prospects, but she had a fire inside her and a mind that could quickly grasp the intricacies of chess. From the moment Phiona followed her older brother Brian to the Sports Outreach Institute where coach Robert Katende taught slum children how to play chess, her life began to change.

Because Phiona knew nothing about chess, the first child she was matched to play against was only four years old. Phiona was already nine and towered over tiny Gloria Nansubuga.

'I don't want to teach that old lady,' said Gloria.

Phiona was embarrassed to play with such a little kid but she was also determined to learn. Day after day she returned until she had learned everything she could from Gloria. It wasn't long before she began to play against the bigger boys.

QUEEN'S GAMBIT

In August 2006, Phiona competed in her very first chess tournament. At first, when she glanced around the hall full of boys playing chess, she thought there had been a mistake. Where were the other girls? But Phiona won three games in the tournament and was awarded a small prize for being the only girl to compete.

Less than a year later, Phiona competed in Uganda's Under 20 national chess championship. Most of the other competitors were in their late teens. Phiona was only 11. At the end of the tournament, she stood shyly waiting to hear who had won. She knew she had played her best but she was astonished when it was announced she was the women's champion. The gold trophy she received was nearly as tall as she was.

In 2009, Phiona took her first trip in an aeroplane when she flew to Sudan to compete in an international chess tournament. She had never travelled outside Uganda, never stayed in a hotel, never even slept in a bed of her own The remote control for the television, the air-conditioning and the flush toilet all seemed like magic.

At the tournament, Phiona played eight games without losing once. Her teammates, two boys from Katwe, were also undefeated. All three Ugandan players were street kids who had worked hard to win their place in the tournament. Sixteen African countries competed, but it was the kids from Katwe who triumphed and were declared tournament champions.

FROM KATWE TO HOLLYWOOD

Winning the all-Africa competition changed Phiona. All of a sudden, a whole new life was made possible through chess. At 14 years of age, Phiona became the youngest member of the Ugandan team to compete at the 2010 Chess Olympiad in Russia. Although Phiona didn't play as well as she would have liked, many people were impressed by her playing and she continued to be invited to compete on the international chess circuit. The Chess Olympiad is held every two years and Phiona has continued to represent Uganda at every Olympiad.

What makes Phiona's story so inspiring is not that she was a chess prodigy like Judit Polgar, but that chess became a way for Phiona to raise herself out of poverty. Chess opened a door into the world and Phiona marched through it into a whole new life.

In 2010, an American sports journalist, Tim Crothers, heard about Phiona through a friend who had read about her in a newsletter from the Sports Outreach Institute. Almost instantly, Crothers knew that Phiona's story would make a fascinating book. He began to visit Uganda to interview Phiona, her family, her coach and all the other children of Katwe who were part of her story.

Crothers's biography of Phiona, *The Queen of Katwe*, was published in 2012. Not long after, producers from Disney Studios read the story and decided it would make a great film. The whole world would hear about the little girl from Katwe.

On 20 September 2016, Phiona attended the Hollywood premiere of *Queen of Katwe*, the movie about her life so far. She sat in the darkened theatre watching a version of her rise to fame play out on the big screen. Her determination to master the game of chess had led her on an amazing journey.

Thanks to all the publicity and her rise to stardom, Phiona was offered a scholarship to study at Northwest University in Ohio, USA. Her old chess coach, Robert Katende, continues to teach chess to the children of Katwe, many of whom have gone on to win championships across the world, including Phiona's very first teacher, Gloria Nansubuga. For the children of Katwe, life is like a complicated chess game that many of them are winning.

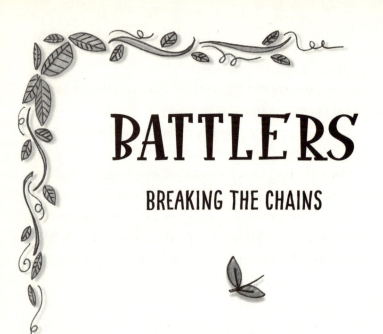

BATTLERS

BREAKING THE CHAINS

Kids who are superstars are hard workers – you have to be to make it to the top. But at least superstar workers get rewarded for all their hard work. Working because you have to is very different to working simply because you love what you do. Kids who are rebels have to look at injustices and challenge them, no matter what, but for most working kids, it can feel too hard to ask questions when their lives are a battle to simply survive. Children have been working to make ends meet for thousands of years. Thinking about how children broke the chains in the past can help build a better future.

PUT THROUGH THE MILL

Lancashire, England, 1799

'Robert, Robert, did you hear the news?' said little Mary Richards as she slid into place at the workhouse dinner table. 'The owner of the great cotton mill in Nottingham, Lamberts, has offered work to all us children. He's going to turn us into proper ladies and gents. There'll be roast beef and plum pudding and we'll have silver watches and the like. The master will even let us ride his horses. An' there'll be plenty of cash to line our pockets with too!'

'Well, I s'pose it'd be better than working as a sweep,' said Robert.

Robert Blincoe was seven years old, the same age as Mary, but he'd already had some experience of the world outside the workhouse. The year before, when he was only six, he'd been sent out to clean chimneys.

'Aye, that was terrible work for you, wasn't it?' said Mary.

'Mmmm, I just couldn't get up the chimneys fast enough. The master – he'd light matches and burn the bottom of my feet trying to hurry me up. But I was too scared of all that blackness. After I got stuck in one chimney and was too afrighted to go up or come down, he sent me back to the workhouse, saying I'd never make a sweep.'

Robert couldn't remember his parents. He and Mary Richards had both lived in St Pancras Workhouse since they were tiny, along with other orphans and homeless poor people who worked there to pay for their keep.

In 1799, a local cotton mill (a factory where raw cotton was spun and turned into cloth) approached the workhouse and struck a deal with the wardens to take over the care of the children until they were 21 years of age. On a sunny summer day, 80 boys and girls aged seven years were loaded into carts that lined up outside the workhouse.

SLOP AND BLACK BREAD

When they reached the mill, the children were herded into a big common room with long narrow tables and wooden benches. Robert and Mary were separated; she to sit with the girls and he with the boys. There was no cloth, no plates, no knives or forks. Robert pushed away his feelings of unease and concentrated on the exciting thought of plum pudding. He'd never eaten it before, but the idea made his mouth water.

A woman came in with a big black pot and ladled thin blue porridge into the bowls. Each child was given a piece of black bread to have with their slop. Robert looked down at his bowl in disgust.

'I can't eat it,' said the boy next to him, 'though I'm right starving.'

The bread was bitter, and so soft that the black dough stuck to the boys' teeth and made them look as if all their teeth had been knocked out. Robert gagged as he forced himself to swallow.

There was a clatter at the door as the apprentices from the mill arrived, girls and boys. They were a thin and scruffy gang; their hair stood on end and they were barefoot. When the overseer nodded, they rushed to a hatch door and jostled each other as a woman opened it. The boys pulled their shirts out and the girls held up their greasy aprons to catch some hot potatoes that were doled out.

'Why, they're like animals!' exclaimed Robert.

The apprentices wolfed down their potatoes and then, seeing the new kids, crowded around the table like a band of ragged starlings.

'Here, out of the way,' said a big boy, as he elbowed Robert to one side. He grabbed Robert's bowl and licked the last drops of porridge from the bottom before snatching up the crusts of the horrid black bread and cramming them into his mouth. Robert watched him with disgust. Little did he know that within a few weeks he would look and behave exactly like this boy.

The boys were shown up two flights of dark winding stairs to their bedrooms. Robert was paired up with the big hungry boy who'd elbowed him at supper. None of the new children were allowed to share with their friends. The bigger boy couldn't wait to get into bed and fell asleep instantly. The stench of oily clothes and the boy's blackened, greasy skin turned Robert's stomach. He curled into a little ball with his back to the big boy and cried himself to sleep.

THE WORKING DAY

The next day Robert was sent to work at 5.30 a.m. The air in the millhouse was thick with dust and his throat and eyes began to sting. All around him, huge machines whirled and roared.

'Well, boy, I'm Mr Smith,' said the overlooker who organised the workers, 'and your job is to collect all the loose cotton that's fallen to the floor.'

After three hours of stooping and gathering, Robert's back began to ache. The stench from the machines and the little fragments of cotton in the air were making him feel sick. He sat down on the floor to rest for a moment.

'Oi, boy, what do you think you're doing?' shouted Mr Smith, cuffing him across the back of his head. 'I won't have any slackers in this mill. Get up and get back to work.'

At midday – after Robert had spent six and a half hours of stooping and gathering – a bell rang somewhere in the cotton mill and the master indicated Robert could stop. He knelt down on the floor with relief.

The work Robert was doing was called scavenging, and it was very dangerous. He would often have to wriggle under the machines on his stomach and sometimes tufts of his hair would be caught and torn out by the whirring machinery. Accidents were especially likely when he was tired. Sometimes the children would be so exhausted from working for over 15 hours a day that they grew drowsy. Then the overlooker would pick them up by their ankles and dip them in a big barrel of cold water that stood in a corner of the room to force them awake.

FOR SHAME

After a few months of scavenging, Robert was promoted to being a winder. He was still so little that they had to place him on a block so he could reach his work. He worked as quickly as he could, but he couldn't wind the cotton fast enough. Mr Smith took to him with a stick and beat him till blood gushed from his nose and mouth. Robert shrieked and raised his arms to protect his head, but the blows kept falling.

'Sir, sir, I'm trying, I'm working as fast as I can,' he wept.

Downstairs, on the ground floor of the cotton mill, a blacksmith named William Palfrey was hammering at his forge when he felt something dripping from the ceiling. He slid his hand across the back of his neck and his palm was red with blood.

'Not again,' he muttered and reached for a crowbar. He

leaped up onto a bench and pounded at the ceiling. 'For shame! For shame! Are you murdering the children?' roared the blacksmith. 'I'll not stand for it, you animals! Stop it up there, or I'll come up and stop you myself!'

Mr Smith stopped the flogging.

'Thank God for William Palfrey,' said one of the other apprentices to Robert as he helped him to his feet. 'If it weren't for him, we'd be beaten even worse. But he goes home to Litton at seven o'clock, and there's no mercy for us then.'

BLOOD AND COTTON

The boys and girls were kept completely separate at the mills, not like at the workhouse where they had often played together. Robert would wave to Mary at lunchtime, but if he tried to talk to her, he got a beating. Robert thought she was still the prettiest girl in the place, no matter how thin she had grown.

They had been at the cotton mill for nearly three years when the accident happened. Mary worked at a machine that drew the cotton out ready for spinning. Clumpy wads of cotton were stretched across a series of frames that moved past her, and Mary's small hands would fly across the moving frames, pushing the loose cotton into place. Underneath the machine was a shaft by which the frames were turned. One evening, Mary's ripped and tatty apron caught in the machinery and drew her with it. Her shrieks rose up above the whirr of the machines.

'Mary!' screamed Robert as he stopped his loom and leaped down from his box. He felt he was running in slow motion as he pushed past the overlooker.

'Mary, Mary,' he cried in agony as he stood helplessly watching his friend whirled round and round in the shaft. It only took a moment but it seemed to last forever. Blood streamed across the floor as Mary was drawn tighter into the works of the machine. Robert covered his ears to block out the sound of her bones snapping, her screams and then the terrible silence as the blood spattered across the frame and the cotton turned red.

'Help her, stop the machinery! Oh God, stop the machinery!' he sobbed, but the machines stopped of their own accord as Mary lay jammed between the shafts and the floor.

For once, everything was quiet in the room. Robert covered his face with his hands as they extracted the little girl from beneath the shaft. Every bone was broken, her head crushed, her body lifeless.

Mary was not quite ten years old.

AFTER THE MILLS

Robert finished his apprenticeship in 1813, and four years he left the mill and set up a small cotton-spinning busines was physically small and crippled by his experiences in the cotton mills; his hands were gnarled and his knees deformed from the long hours of standing at the loom.

Despite bad luck with fire, debt and other misfortune, Robert kept battling. He married, had three children and fought to make a good life for each of them. He swore that all his kids would get a good education and never be forced to the mills. 'I'd rather send them to Australia than to the mills,' he said. (Australia was an unknown wilderness in those days, a prison colony at the edge of the world.) One of Robert's sons went on to graduate from Queen's College, Cambridge and became a minister. Robert died in 1860 in the home of his daughter.

Robert Blincoe gave evidence in special investigations into child labour in England in 1832. The story of his childhood was told in the newspapers, and the public was shocked to realise what bad conditions so many children worked under. Thousands of children died or were crippled for life from working in the cotton mills of England, often referred to as 'the dark Satanic mills'. There was a campaign to improve the lives of working children. Gradually laws were introduced in Britain (and Australia) that prevented adults from employing children for long hours or in dangerous occupations.

Compulsory schooling was introduced in Britain, America, Canada and Australia from around 1870 onwards. Getting into the classroom liberated millions of children from the horrors of factory treadmills. Despite this, it wasn't until the early part of the twentieth century that child labour began to be less common in Australia, America, Britain and Europe.

Despite improved conditions for children in some places, people in richer countries gave little thought to the fact that there were still millions of children working in factories and sweatshops in other parts of the world. In the early 1990s, one boy would begin to change that and became a hero to millions of working children.

CHILDHOOD IN CHAINS

Muridke, Pakistan, 1992

Iqbal's voice dropped to a whisper as the overseer walked past him.

'So, we'll go together then?' he asked as he tied another small knot.

'Yes, tomorrow morning,' muttered Mustafa. 'I just hope no one finds out about it.'

The overseer shouted at them and they turned back to their work at the looms.

The air was filled with dust and tiny flecks of wool. All day the factory echoed with the sound of the looms clacking as the boys wove rugs in beautiful colours to be sent to showrooms around the world.

Somewhere in the factory, one of the new little boys was screaming. He had hurt his finger and the master had forced him to put it into hot oil to toughen his skin. If any of the kids complained or were too slow they were beaten or hung upside down as a punishment.

Iqbal knew that tomorrow a meeting was to be held in Sheikhupura, and Ehsan Ullah Khan, the president of the Bonded Labor Liberation Front (BLLF), was going to speak to the bonded labourers who were brave enough to attend. Iqbal knew that he would be in trouble if he took a day off work without permission. The master would probably chain him to his loom again, but he was prepared to take the risk.

DEBT SLAVE

Iqbal Masih had been sold into bonded labour when he was only five. His mother was ill and needed money for an operation but she had no one to turn to, as Iqbal's father had left when Iqbal was only a few years old. Iqbal's mother borrowed 5000 rupees (about $100 Australian dollars at that time) from the carpet manufacturer, but it was Iqbal who would have to pay the money back.

From the day his mother took out the loan, Iqbal was forced to work at least 12 hours each day, six days every week, for which he was paid the equivalent of only one dollar per week.

When the factory was busy meeting an order, he could be at the loom for up to 20 hours a day and sometimes he worked seven days per week. If he made mistakes, he was fined and the fine was added to his debt. His mother's health was still poor and more small loans were added to the original one. No matter how fast Iqbal worked, he could never repay the money his mother had borrowed. By the time he was ten years old, the amount he owed to the carpet-maker had more than doubled - it could take him the rest of his life to repay the debt.

CRY FOR FREEDOM

The boys hurried through the busy streets of Sheikhupura to reach the meeting place. It had taken them an hour to get to the town by trolley from Muridke. Hundreds of people were milling about in the square listening to Ehsan Ullah Khan talk about the fight for justice for the workers of Pakistan.

Iqbal and his friends could hardly see the speaker above the crowd of grown-ups. They were terrified someone would report them to the factory owner, so they lowered their heads and listened to Ehsan Ullah Khan telling them how whole families sometimes worked for generations to pay off small loans, and bonded labourers who inherited their fathers' debts were forced to sell their own children. They were little better than slaves. 'The Abolition of Bonded Labour Act' had been passed by the government in March of 1992. The workers had to join together to make the government keep its promises and fight corruption.

Iqbal had always felt the way things were at the carpet factory was wrong. Now he lifted his head and gazed fiercely at the stage, as he realised that what had happened to him was actually illegal, and that he had rights he had never dreamt of.

Ehsan Ullah Khan looked out across the crowd. Something about the small boy staring up at him caught his attention. As the next speaker took the stage, he made his way through the crowd to the boy with the burning eyes.

'Would you like to go up on the stage and say a few words about how it is for you?' asked Khan.

For a moment Iqbal hesitated, before nodding his head.

'Yes,' he replied in the wheezy voice of an old man. (Years of working in the dusty carpet factory had damaged Iqbal's lungs.) 'I will tell my story, but not just my story – I will tell how it is for the children.'

Everyone fell completely quiet as Iqbal's small voice described the terrible conditions of the carpet-weaving children, and asked for help to end their suffering. It was a short speech and when he finished there was silence. For a moment, Iqbal thought no one had heard him, but suddenly the crowd burst into spontaneous applause and shouts of praise echoed in his ears.

Iqbal returned to Muridke that evening, his head full of ideas and his heart full of hope. When the BLLF sent him a copy of 'The Abolition of Bonded Labour Act', Iqbal presented it to his former master as his 'letter of freedom'. He never returned to work as a carpet weaver.

A DREAM BECOMES REALITY

By the time Iqbal was 12 he had moved to Lahore to attend one of the BLLF free schools. On weekends he would go back to Muridke to visit his mother, who worked as a cleaner, and his little sister Sabia.

Iqbal loved school and worked so hard that he passed two grades each year. He had already decided that he wanted to grow up to be a lawyer so he could fight for the rights of other kids. He was often asked to speak at BLLF rallies. His speeches were reprinted in local newspapers and his reputation as a passionate speaker and a crusader for human rights began to grow.

In the two years after Iqbal escaped from the carpet-weaving factory, thousands of other children, inspired by his courage, made a break for freedom. Human rights groups and labour organisations arranged co-ordinated raids on factories that were exploiting their employees. With a couple of years, over 3000 Pakistani kids were freed from forced labour in carpet, textile and brick factories, leather tanneries and steelworks. Dozens of factories were forced to close as a result.

SNOW, ICE AND FRIENDSHIP

Lidköping, Sweden, 1994

Iqbal reached down into the soft white snow and scooped some into his hands. He waited until the other kids came out of the school hall and into the playground, took aim and threw the snow at Erik Rydstedt. Erik let out a whoop and wrestled him to the ground, pushing snow down Iqbal's collar. The two boys collapsed in a heap of laughter as the other kids gathered around them. Even though Iqbal couldn't speak Swedish, he knew how to share a joke.

Iqbal had been in Sweden for nearly a month but he still couldn't get over how friendly everyone was and how at home he felt. A whole new world of opportunities was opening up for Iqbal. Groups of schoolkids from Lidkoping had already visited him in Pakistan and now he had a chance to see how they lived.

Erik planned to come to Lahore after Christmas. He was just one of hundreds of Swedish kids involved in a group called Youth Against Slavery. Along with their teachers they were committed to helping the BLLF in its fight against child labour.

Iqbal had flown to Stockholm at the end of October to speak at a conference and receive a tribute from the International Labour Organisation. He had become an international figure and everyone who heard him speak was impressed

In December, the sporting footwear company, Reebok, awarded its annual 'Youth in Action' human rights award to Iqbal. He flew from Sweden to the USA to receive the award, give speeches and to meet with politicians and celebrities. He also visited a secondary school and met kids his own age. The visit was destined to change the lives of countless children.

SHARING THE DREAM

Broad Meadows Middle School is in Quincy, a suburb of Boston, Massachusetts. The seventh- and eighth-graders were studying the Universal Declaration of Human Rights, so they knew how important Iqbal's work was, but nothing could really prepare them for the impact his words would have on them. Through a translator, he told them of his life as a child labourer.

'The carpet owners used to tell me that the rugs we were making – that were stained with our blood – were for Americans; that it was the Americans who were making them force us to work like beasts. I thought, "Who are these people, these Americans? They must be demons!" I'm glad that I came here and found you don't have little horns and tails sticking out at the back,' said Iqbal.

Amanda Loos, Jennifer Brundige and Amy Papile were in the audience. They laughed, but they felt ashamed that other Americans were buying the rugs.

Seeing Iqbal had an even bigger impact on them than just reading about him. Iqbal's growth had been stunted by his years of hard labour – he barely came up to their shoulders. The children stood on tables so they could see him as he sat on a chair at the front of their classroom.

Iqbal was so small his feet didn't even touch the ground. 'Carpet factory owners prefer children because our tiny fingers make the smallest, tightest knots. And also because they can control us – they are so much bigger and think they can trick us into believing that they have a right to treat us badly,' said Iqbal. 'If we don't know our rights, it is very difficult for us to fight back because we are so afraid. But I'm not scared of the owner any more – now he's afraid of me!'

Iqbal held up a small carpet knife for the kids to see. 'I used to use this tool in my work on the looms. I want to see the children of my country holding pencils in their hands, not these. One day I would like to be to my country, Pakistan, as Abraham Lincoln was to America. I want to fight to end slavery. My dream is to end child labour for all the children of the world.'

After he had finished speaking the kids crowded around him and each gave him a small gift – bubblegum, stickers, friendship bracelets, hundreds of little souvenirs of his visit to them; even a backpack to put it all in.

When he went home to Pakistan, he stuck some of the pictures and gifts that the children had given him on the wall beside his bed.

LOSING IQBAL

Amanda came inside and played back the messages on the answering machine. When she heard Jen's message, she felt hot with anger. She grabbed the phone and called her friend.

'Jen, that was a really cruel joke – pretending that Iqbal is dead.'

'I'm not joking,' replied Jen. 'It's serious – read the front page of the newspaper. This is what it says: "On Easter Sunday, 16 April 1995, Iqbal Masih, twelve-year-old anti–child labour campaigner, was shot dead. He was riding a bicycle with his cousins outside his grandmother's house." Someone opened fire on them with a twelve-bore shotgun – one of the cousins was hit as well. Within minutes, Iqbal was dead.'

Amanda clutched the phone and felt tears burning her eyes.

'Amanda?' said Jen. 'C'mon over to my house. I need you here. Please.'

Amanda grabbed her backpack and ran out the door. The cold spring air made her cheeks flush pink as she raced down the street. When she burst into Jen's kitchen, she wanted to shout with anger, but one look at her friend told her Jen had been crying.

'Oh, Jen,' she said. They folded their arms around each other and cried.

THE POWER OF SEVENTH-GRADERS

The next day was a public holiday, but 30 kids met at the school along with their teacher, Ron Adams. Everyone held hands for a moment of silence and remembered Iqbal.

They hugged each other and spoke softly about him, remembering little things – how tiny his hand had felt when they shook it, how much fire was in his small body. As they talked about him, their anger grew and the fire was lit inside them, too.

Ron Adams got all the students to write down their thoughts.

Suddenly Amy looked up. 'Why don't we do something?' she said. 'Something that will make a real difference. Why don't we build a school in Pakistan?'

'What? Yeah, right,' said Amanda and rolled her eyes. 'Amy, you are such a dreamer.'

'No, really. Why don't we build a school for Iqbal? We all know how to write letters,' Amy began. 'And we know how to send emails. Well, I think we should write to everyone – to all the other middle schools in America, to senators, to the mayor, to everyone we can think of. Ask for donations. Ask for twelve dollars from every seventh-grade class in every school. Most seventh-graders are twelve years old. So we can ask every class of seventh-graders to make a donation – twelve dollars from each student. Iqbal was twelve when he came to visit us, twelve when he won the Reebok award, and he was twelve when he died. It's symbolic; it makes you think of Iqbal.'

The room exploded with excited conversation as everyone offered suggestions of how the idea might become a reality.

'Okay, slow down,' said Mr Adams. 'I want you guys to go home tonight and write down all your ideas. When you've got it in writing we'll have another look at it.'

'He thinks we're going to forget about this,' whispered Amanda.

'He thinks we're crazy,' said Amy.

'He just doesn't know what we can do,' said Jen. 'Never underestimate the power of seventh-graders.'

A SCHOOL FOR IQBAL

Amanda, Jen and Amy swung into action. Dozens of other kids joined the campaign. They wrote thousands of letters and emails, organised fundraising events and made contact with supporters across America. Seventh-graders from all over the USA emailed their support, made donations and asked how they could help. The campaign leaders worked weekends and through their holidays. By the first anniversary of Iqbal's death, in April 1996, the kids at Broad Meadows Middle School had raised over US$100 000. At last they had enough money to open a school in Iqbal's memory.

The kids approached 300 different non-governmental organisations from around the world. Twelve of these replied explaining how they would run a school if the kids chose them to organise it.

In November 1996, the children of Broad Meadows Middle School chose a Pakistani organisation called Sudhaar, which means 'hope' in Urdu – the language that Iqbal spoke.

Sudhaar is a non-government organisation that works with the people of Punjab – the province in Pakistan that was Iqbal's home. By December of 1997, 278 working kids from some of the poorest families in Kasur – a city in Pakistan – were attending the school. They were aged between four and 12 years of age, and many of them were liberated bonded labourers. The donations from Broad Meadows Middle School helped hundreds of kids like Iqbal escape child labour. Eventually, Sudhaar expanded its programs to open 780 literacy centres in Pakistan over the next 20 years.

A BULLET CAN'T KILL A DREAM

Amanda, Jen and Amy knew that their commitment to fighting for children's rights wouldn't stop. True to their promise to Iqbal, the kids of Quincy continued to think about ways they could help bring education to other children. In 1998, students at Broad Meadows School partnered with other schools to set up a new organisation called ODW-USA (Operation Day's Work USA). Every year the students raise funds for a particular project, and since ODW-USA's formation they have helped thousands of other children.

Iqbal inspired people all around the world to work to end child labour. Dozens of schools have been opened in his memory. There are also prizes, plazas and even sporting events that bear his name. His memory was honoured again in 2000 when he received the World Children's Honorary Award.

A THOUSAND NEW IQBALS

Although the carpet manufacturers denied responsibility for Iqbal's death and a local farmer was charged with the murder, many people believe Iqbal was killed because of his campaign against employing children in carpet factories. Iqbal had received death threats in the months before the shooting because he refused to be silent.

At Iqbal's funeral, hundreds of children followed his open coffin through the streets of Muridke. But the children of Pakistan were not alone in mourning the loss of Iqbal. On the first anniversary of Iqbal's death, thousands of Swedish children gathered in the main town square of Lidköping to remember the boy who had touched their lives. Erik Rydstedt gave a speech while other kids from Youth Against Slavery sold balloons to raise money to help the BLLF. At the sound of a trumpet fanfare, the children released their balloons into the morning sky.

All around the world, kids remembered Iqbal and made vows to follow in his footsteps. In Lahore, a small Pakistani girl stood on the steps of Government House, facing the camera of an international filmmaker, and said, 'The day Iqbal died, a thousand new Iqbals sprang up to take his place.'

JOINING THE BATTLE

Craig Kielburger spread the *Toronto Star* newspaper out in front of him at the breakfast table and reached for the sugar bowl. As his eyes skimmed the page he noticed a picture of a small boy smiling up at him – a boy who had just been murdered.

Like Iqbal, Craig was 12 years old, but unlike Iqbal he had a comfortable, safe life. He lived with his family in a leafy suburb of Toronto, Canada, had his own bedroom and went to school every day. He had thought child labour was a thing of the past – that it had ended at least 100 years ago – but reading about Iqbal's life made him realise he was terribly wrong.

Craig started reading everything he could find about child labour and giving talks on the issue at his school. With a group of friends, he set up an organisation called Free the Children, and together they started to write letters and organise fundraising events.

One of their first campaigns was to collect 3000 signatures calling for the release of the imprisoned child labour activist, Kailash Satyarthi. Craig and his team put the petition in a shoebox and wrapped it in brown paper. Then they sent it to the Prime Minister of India. When Satyarthi was finally released from prison he said, 'It was one of the most powerful actions taken on my behalf, and for me, definitely the most memorable.'

Several months later, the International Program for the Elimination of Child Labour suggested that Craig's group should send someone to Asia to investigate what was really going on there. Craig managed to talk his parents into letting him go. A friend of the family, who was from Bengal in India and spoke Hindi and Bengali (two of the languages of India), went with him and together they spent seven weeks touring Nepal, India, Pakistan, Thailand and Bangladesh.

Craig met a girl in a metals factory who showed him where her arms and legs had been severely burnt by hot metal. A boy from a fireworks factory told Craig that when he cut himself his employers put phosphorus in the wound so it would be burnt shut. Craig spoke with an eight-year-old girl who worked in a recycling factory in India sorting syringes, with no protective clothing. She walked barefoot over a floor that was strewn with used needles.

Both boys and girls showed Craig the scars that were all over their bodies from punishments they had received. One boy had been branded across the throat with a hot iron for trying to help his brother escape. Craig listened carefully and grew even more determined to help.

THE LONG ROAD HOME

Craig met people from across Asia who were fighting for change. One group that had organised a raid on a carpet factory invited Craig to accompany 23 children back to their village. The children had been tricked into working for a carpet manufacturer and were taken far from their homes with promises of being given fair wages and good working conditions.

On the trip back to their village the children began to sing.

'What are they singing?' asked Craig.

'They are singing, *We are free. We are going home,*' said the translator as the jeep splashed along a muddy track.

One nine-year-old boy, Munilal, told Craig how when he had cried for his mother at the carpet factory, he was beaten. So every night he had spoken to her in his dreams. When they reached the village, Munilal saw his mother in the street and leaped from the jeep and ran to her. With a cry of joy she threw her arms around his small thin body. Craig knew that Munilal would no longer have to search for his mother in his dreams, but Craig's dream – to help kids like Munilal – was only just beginning.

A VOICE FOR THE CHILDREN

Like Iqbal, Craig proved to be a persuasive speaker. While he was in India, he organised press conferences, attended rallies and gave interviews describing all the things he was finding out.

The Canadian prime minister was travelling in Asia at the same time as Craig. He decided he should meet with this kid that everyone was talking about. Craig convinced him that he had to take action. The Canadian government agreed to donate C$700 000 to the International Program for the Elimination of Child Labour (IPEC) and set up committees to examine ways of preventing exploitation of children both at home and in the countries that Canada traded with. Craig became an international spokesperson for children's rights.

FROM FREE TO WE

Free the Children began to grow at an incredible speed. Craig quickly enlisted the help of his older brother, Marc Kielburger, and together they worked to create an international charity network.

Craig and Marc soon realised that freeing children from factory work wasn't going to solve the children's problems if they were forced to live in utter poverty. Free the Children became the basis for a new charity called WE. Through WE, the Kielburgers and their supporters have set up programs that have helped to lift an estimated 100 million people out of poverty. The brothers developed a philosophy that if they could help whole communities, they could genuinely free the children. Their charity focuses on helping communities to access education, clean water and sanitation, health care, secure ways to find food and new sources of income.

Craig believes in the power of education and has two university degrees. He has also received 15 honorary degrees for his work in education and human rights. His first book was published when he was 16 years old and since then he's written many other books as well as hundreds of articles for magazines and newspapers. Craig has been awarded The Order of Canada, the Nelson Mandela Freedom Medal and the World's Children's prize for his work helping others.

BIG CHANGES START SMALL

The story of Iqbal Masih led Craig Kielburger to start a global movement, and Craig's story has inspired thousands of young people. But every movement starts small, with one person looking at ways that they can make a difference, and sometimes a single act of kindness can be the start of something much bigger.

THE MAN IN THE RUBBISH BIN

Hawkesbury, New South Wales, Autumn 2011

Cassidy Strickland couldn't believe her eyes. She pressed her face against the front window and peered into the dark night. Someone was outside her house. Someone in a hoodie with an old dog beside him. As her eyes adjusted to the darkness, she saw that a man was rummaging through the rubbish bin. It took her a moment to realise that he was searching for food. How could anyone in her neighbourhood be so hungry that they'd eat food out of a bin?

Cassidy was only eight years old and in Grade Two at her local primary school but she knew that what she was seeing was wrong. She ran into the kitchen where her mum, Linda, was sipping a cup of coffee.

'Mum!' said Cassidy. 'There's a man outside our house eating food out of our rubbish bin!'

'Perhaps he's homeless,' said Linda.

'But that's terrible! You'd have to be starving to eat rubbish.'

'What should we do about it, Cass?' said Linda.

'Feed him!' said Cassidy.

'How about fruit and sandwiches?' asked Linda, hurrying to the fridge.

Together, Linda and Cassidy stood behind the screen door of their home and called out to the man.

'Can we bring you some sandwiches and a cup of coffee, mister?' said Cassidy.

'Or a piece of fruit?' called Linda.

The man looked up, startled. His clothes were dirty and his face unshaven. For a moment, he hesitated. Then he ran across the road with his dog and disappeared into the trees along the riverbank.

Cassidy turned to Linda, looking worried. 'Why did he run away?' she asked. 'We only wanted to help him.'

'He was probably embarrassed,' said Linda.

'He shouldn't have to feel that way. No one should be ashamed of being hungry.'

Cassidy stared out into the night, imagining what it must be like to sleep by the river and to have nowhere to call home.

'I want to do something to help him, Mum,' said Cassidy. 'It's awful that there are people around here who are homeless and don't have anywhere to go or enough to eat. It's not fair that they have to eat out of rubbish bins.'

THE COMMUNITY KITCHEN

That Wednesday night, Cassidy and her mum cooked up a big pot of soup and took it to the local community kitchen in Hawkesbury. They helped out by serving food, setting and clearing tables, and washing dishes.

Hawkesbury is a city of 65 000 people, situated 50 kilometres from central Sydney. Although the city offers a range of services to people in trouble, homelessness can sometimes be invisible. In 2016, more than 100 000 Australians were estimated to be homeless and that number has only grown since. People of all ages can wind up having nowhere safe to live at different times in their lives because of financial and other problems. Community kitchens are important places that help homeless people by offering them a free meal and somewhere they can find friendly company without being judged.

One day, after Cassidy had been helping out at the community kitchen for some time, she noticed a sign by the front door that said the kitchen was closed on weekends. Up until then, she'd always come in through the back door.

'Mum, did you know that the community kitchen is closed on weekends? What do all the homeless people do then? Where do they eat if this place is closed?' asked Cassidy. 'We have to do more, Mum.' Linda agreed.

That Wednesday, Cassidy told everyone in the community kitchen to meet her and her mum in the park on the banks of the Hawkesbury River on Saturday night.

SUNSHINE OR RAIN

On Saturday morning Cassidy and Linda went shopping. Linda used her own money to buy food. Then, at home, Cassidy cooked alongside her mum and they packed meals into containers. The first night only seven people turned up, but soon word spread and more and more people began arriving to enjoy Cassidy and Linda's meals.

One Saturday, Cassidy counted over 65 people in the park lining up to receive the takeaway containers of homemade food she'd prepared with her mother. There were families with children and babies, old people and teenagers. Even the man who had run away from her when she found him searching in the rubbish bins turned up and thanked Cassidy and Linda for the food. His name was Froggy and he'd decided Cassidy was a hero. No one went hungry when Cassidy and Linda were there to help, but Cassidy began to realise that a lot of the homeless people weren't just hungry; they were also lonely.

Cassidy and Linda began organising sit-down dinners in the park, as well as takeaway meals. When the community kitchen closed down for a month across the summer holidays, Cassidy and Linda went to the park three nights a week, in sunshine or rain, supplying food for the homeless. Luckily, people started to hear about their good work and donations of gift cards and new volunteers joined them.

One Christmas Eve, it was raining so heavily that they wondered if anyone would bother to turn up at the meeting place on the riverbank.

'Wow! It's raining cats and dogs,' said Linda, as she and Cassidy ran from the house to the car with armloads of supplies.

'Check out the lightning!' said Cassidy.

'Maybe it's not worth going out, Cass,' said Linda. 'Most people are probably sheltering from the rain somewhere.'

'But what if someone does turn up?' said Cassidy. 'And we're not there?'

'You're a good noodle,' said Linda. 'Of course, you're right. We're not going to disappoint anyone, even if it's only one person.'

As they drove through the pouring rain and turned towards

their usual parking spot, another bolt of lightning crashed onto the riverbank.

'Look, Mum!' said Cassidy. 'That tree, the one near where we set up, the lightning's struck it and split it in two!'

And then they saw the people. Twenty-five soaking-wet homeless people were standing in water up to their ankles, hoping that Cassidy and Linda would turn up to be with them on Christmas Eve.

Cassidy and Linda swore they'd always brave the storms to help people. Even if it was Cassidy's birthday or Mother's Day, Christmas Day or any other special occasion, Linda and Cassidy fed people on the riverbank. No matter what the weather was like, the mother-daughter team made sure no one in Hawkesbury went hungry.

HAWKESBURY HELPING HANDS

In 2013, Cassidy and Linda set up a registered charity called Hawkesbury Helping Hands that supplied not only food but emergency services to homeless people as well. By 2018, Cassidy's original simple act of generosity had created an organisation with over 25 volunteers that provided over 300 free lunches, three regular dinner services, and six breakfast services. They also helped provide warm clothing, bedding and other services to give people dignity.

When Cassidy was in Year Eight at Windsor High School, she also helped set up a Breakfast Club so that no student in her school would go hungry. By the time she was in Year Ten, Cassidy was getting up extra early to serve toast, cereal, fruit juice and even doughnuts and bagels to kids who might miss out on breakfast if their families couldn't afford to supply them. Wherever she sees people in need, Cassidy is moved to reach out to them and help.

'Everyone is equal,' said Cassidy. 'And everyone deserves to be treated equally, with dignity and respect.'

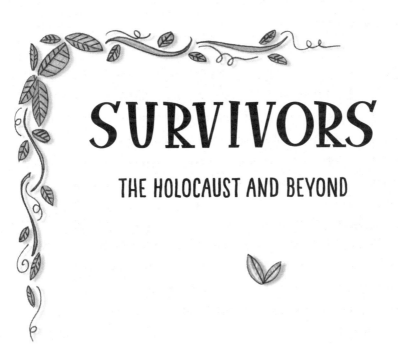

SURVIVORS

THE HOLOCAUST AND BEYOND

When adults fight, it's hard on kids. But when those fights are between adults in government, kids wind up suffering big time. Every child caught in a conflict zone is in danger whether they're simply surviving or being forced to fight. Despite everyone knowing it is wrong to turn kids into soldiers, as many as 300 000 kids under 18 are fighting in conflicts around the world in over 40 different places. The average age of a child soldier is 12, but children as young as five are being forced to fight in some countries.

It might sound like nothing but bad news, but there are some bright candles being lit in the darkness. Fewer people are dying in wars now than in the middle of the twentieth century, and many people around the world are campaigning to free children from war.

When World War II ended in 1945, the United Nations was

formed. As an organisation, it has written many important documents about how to make a better world for everyone. For kids, the most important one of all is the Convention on the Rights of the Child. It lists the rights of children that every country should observe and states that: *Governments must do everything they can to protect and care for children affected by war.*

During World War II, which was fought between 1939 and 1945, millions of children were murdered and made to suffer in wars that raged around the world. But one way kids fought back was with spirit. Even if they couldn't outshoot the grown-ups and could only occasionally outsmart them, kids could always try and outlast them.

A terrible part of World War II was the murder of the Jewish people in Europe – especially Jewish kids. Over 1.5 million Jewish children were murdered during the Holocaust just because they were Jews, as well as 4.5 million Jewish grown-ups.

As well as the six million Jews who died in the Holocaust, five million other civilians were murdered. Anyone who didn't fit Adolf Hitler's idea of what a German should be was in trouble. Anyone with different beliefs and different ways of looking at the world – and that included kids – was at risk.

AREK'S WAR

Arek Hersh stood in the backyard of his cousin's house, looking across the fence at the golden fields of maize. He was ten years old and glad to be in a place that felt so peaceful.

Arek's family had come to the village of Zdunska Wola hoping it would be safer than their home in Sieradz, close to the German border. A few days earlier, on 1 September 1939, the German army had invaded Poland.

Suddenly, Arek heard a roar overhead. A German bomber swooped low over his cousin's house, then another and another. The noise was deafening. The planes began dive-bombing the village, dropping bombs everywhere.

People poured out of the houses in panic and began running in all directions. Arek ran into the fields of maize to hide.

'Arek, Arek, where are you?' he heard his parents calling in panic.

'Here, I'm here,' he called back, but no one heard his small voice above the noise of bombs and gunfire.

'Arek,' called his brother Tovia. 'Arek!'

Arek leaped to his feet as the planes swooped towards him, firing their guns into the maize. He headed for the road but a family with three children lay there dying beside their horse and cart. Terrified, Arek changed direction and ran back towards his cousin's house.

Everything went quiet. The planes had gone.

SLAVE LABOUR

Eventually, Arek and his family made their way to Lodz, where they hoped they would be safe. But the Germans arrived in Lodz on 8 September 1939. Thousands of soldiers marched into the town in long columns.

Jewish men were kicked and beaten in the streets, and

sometimes the soldiers cut their beards off to ridicule them. Jewish families had their possessions confiscated. Arek's father decided to take his family back to Sieradz, but they found their home had been plundered. Nowhere was safe now that the Germans occupied the whole country.

In the week of his eleventh birthday, Arek was caught by the Germans and forced to dig up the bodies of German soldiers who had been killed in the fighting, so they could be placed in coffins. The bodies were horribly wounded and decayed. Arek felt sick but he was forced to keep working.

Jewish schools were closed and shopkeepers were instructed to refuse to sell food to the Jews. All the Jews were rounded up and forced to live in only one part of the town. Arek's father and brother barely managed to avoid being taken away for slave labour. They thought Arek would be safe because he was so young, but he was seized in their place and sent along with several hundred older men and boys to a 'labour camp' at Otoczno.

At the camp hundreds of Jewish men and boys were crammed into filthy barracks. They were given almost no food and made to work 14 hours a day.

The men were often beaten and punished for almost no reason. Arek saw men hanged because they had tried to steal a single potato. Sometimes he had to cut down the bodies of the murdered men.

One day, after Arek had been at the camp for several months, the commandant looked down at the tiny emaciated boy. Arek was the youngest child in the camp, and he was so weak from starvation that he had little strength left.

'You, I'm sending you home,' said the commandant.

Of 900 Jews sent to the slave labour camp at Otoczno, only 11 survived. Arek was one of them.

THE LODZ GHETTO

Arek was happy to be back with his mother, but their troubles were not over. On 14 August 1942, at eight in the morning, the Jews of Sieradz were rounded up again. Only those who were useful would be taken to labour camps. For the rest, certain death lay ahead in the terrible concentration camps and death camps that had been built throughout Poland. Arek prayed that his older brother and sister, who were fit and healthy, would be chosen to work. Even his mother had a chance – she was still young. Arek had little hope for himself – he knew he was too small and unskilled to be chosen.

Fourteen hundred Jews crushed into a church waiting to be interrogated by German SS officers. Although he was only 13, Arek decided he would pretend he had a trade.

'What's your trade?' barked an officer.

'*Schneider* (tailor),' said Arek, drawing himself up to his full height and trying to look confident. The SS officer glanced at his small body and sent him back into the church.

Inside, his mother, brother Tovia and sister Itka were waiting. They too had been rejected. Only 150 of the fittest-looking adults and teenagers were chosen as labourers. Not one of Arek's relatives was among them.

'At least we shall all be together,' thought Arek. 'That is some small thing to be happy about.'

It was hot in the church, and after a while Arek grew thirsty. His mother gave him a metal pan.

'Go and ask the guard for water,' she said.

As he approached the gate an SS officer called out to him.

'Boy, what are you?' he shouted.

'A tailor,' replied Arek, without thinking why he was asked.

'Out!' bawled the officer.

Before Arek realised what was happening, he found himself standing with the 150 people who were to be saved. He was horrified. They were marched away from the church.

Arek spent the long night crying. Everyone tried to assure him that his family would be safe at another camp, but Arek had seen enough at Otoczno to know that the Germans showed no mercy. Later he discovered that everyone who had stayed behind at the church had been murdered.

In the morning, soldiers came and took away everything that the working Jews carried with them – all Arek was left with were six photos of his family and the metal pan his mother had given him. The next day they were sent to the Lodz ghetto. Seventy thousand Jewish people from all over Poland were crammed into a few city blocks and made to work in all sorts of factories for the Germans. After six months of living on the streets, growing thinner and hungrier, Arek found a home in the only orphanage left in the ghetto. The children in the orphanage were starving and they had to work every day like the adults, but they looked forward to being together in the evenings.

Arek became especially close friends with Genia. Genia was a beautiful girl with big brown eyes, curly black hair and a warm smile. During the day, Genia worked in a leather factory; at night Arek would sit with her as she told stories to the younger children in the orphanage. She loved to take care of the smallest kids. Like Arek, Genia had lost all her family.

In August 1944, the Lodz ghetto was marked for destruction. The Germans were losing the war but they were still determined to destroy the Jews. The people of the ghetto were to be rounded up and taken in trains to death camps at Chelmno and Auschwitz.

TRAIN TO HELL

The order came for the orphanage to close and 185 children were assembled outside it. They were all small and frail from years of living on a starvation diet. They marched through the streets to the railway station.

Arek knew how thin their chances of survival were, but he pulled himself together and helped Genia comfort the younger children.

So many bodies were crammed tightly into wagons on the train that the passengers could barely breathe. It grew hotter and hotter. Some people, already weak and ill from years of starvation and overwork, died standing up. A few kind people shared the water that they had brought with them, but there was nothing to eat. All day the wagon rattled on. Genia trembled with fear. Arek stroked her face and took her hand in his.

'It's all right, Genia. I have been to a camp before and I am still alive,' he said as he squeezed her hand tightly. Genia grew calmer, but Arek knew they were heading into darkness.

AUSCHWITZ

Early next morning the train stopped. The children were herded
down a long concrete ramp. Beyond lay the camp, surrounded by
barbed wire and electric fences. Guards were hitting people and
shouting at them. Everywhere was noise, distress and confusion.
Arek noticed that the Germans were separating people into two
rows. The people on the left were mostly old people and small
children, many of them from the orphanage. Arek realised they
were doomed. He drew himself up to his full height and tried to
look strong. The SS men barely glanced at him before pointing
him over to the left. Numb with terror, Arek joined the row of
those condemned to die.

Suddenly there was a commotion as a scuffle broke out.

Instinctively, while the guard's attention was elsewhere, Arek
stepped across the line and into the right-hand row. No one
noticed.

Minutes later he shuffled through the gates and into the
camp – Auschwitz.

Over the next year, Arek was to witness unspeakable brutality.
His friends would die around him. Genia was murdered on the
first day, some died of disease, others of starvation.

By April 1945, it was clear to everyone that the Germans
were losing the war, but the killing didn't stop. As the Germans
retreated from the advancing Russian army, Arek and other boys
from the camps were rounded up again and taken on one last
terrible journey to the ghetto at Theresienstadt.

BEGINNING OF THE END

The train came to a stop and everyone was ordered off. As the guards watched, Arek and his friend Yakub made a small fire and cooked themselves grass. It gave them a stomach-ache but staved off their hunger. Afterwards, they went down to the river to drink. For no reason, the guards opened fire. Ten prisoners were killed. Then they were all loaded back onto the death-train.

All the boys were suffering from severe malnutrition. Everyone was crawling with lice. Every few hours, another person on the train would die. Sometimes Arek wondered what it was that kept him alive.

All night they stood crammed into the wagons while anti-aircraft guns were fired from the train. They had been travelling for nine days. The place they had left had already been liberated by the Americans, and yet they were still prisoners.

A guard opened the side of the wagon and stared in at the boys.

'It won't be long,' said the guard. 'You will soon be free.'

'What do you mean?' asked Arek.

'Hitler is dead,' said the guard.

Arek could hardly believe what he was hearing, but next time the train stopped, a young Czechoslovakian policeman offered them bread. When an SS guard went to hit one of the boys, the young policeman said, 'If you touch this child, I will shoot you.' The SS guard walked away. Arek knew they would soon be saved.

THERESIENSTADT

Theresienstadt was both a ghetto and a concentration camp. Arek and his companions were taken to a crowded bunkhouse where they collapsed with exhaustion. A few days after arriving, Arek woke to the sounds of footsteps and shouting in the street. Climbing up to look out the window, he saw jeeps filled with Russian soldiers arriving and hundreds of people running towards them. People were dancing in the street. Arek realised he wasn't dreaming.

'Wake up! Wake up!' he shouted. 'The Russians have entered the ghetto! We're free!'

He and the other boys in his hut dressed as quickly as they could and raced out into the street. Arek's heart was so full with happiness his chest hurt. He could hardly talk. One of the other boys came back to the bunkhouse with smoked meat, cheese, butter and chocolate. It was the first time Arek had seen such food in over five years. He ate a tiny piece of chocolate. It tasted even better than he remembered.

The next morning the Germans were rounded up.

Arek went to watch. The Russians had given the Jewish people 24 hours to do whatever they wanted to the Germans. Arek stopped an SS captain and asked if he could have his knapsack.

'But it has my food in it!' shouted the captain.

'We have been starved by you for five years,' replied Arek.

The captain continued to argue but a Russian soldier pointed his gun at him.

'You are not the masters any more,' he said. 'Give the boy what he asks.'

The captain glared at Arek.

'If I asked this soldier, he would shoot you,' said Arek. 'But we are not murderers, like you.'

Arek was 16 years old when Theresienstadt was liberated. In the last five years, he had borne witness to the worst horrors that man can inflict upon man. Most people who live to be 90 never have to endure what Arek endured. Luck, courage and persistence allowed him to live to tell his story.

After the war England declared it would take in 1000 young survivors of the camps and make a new home for them in Britain. Despite the fact that over 1.5 million children had passed through the gates of Auschwitz and other death camps, only 732 child survivors could be found to take up the offer. Arek was one of them. He settled in England permanently and built a new life for himself.

EVA'S STORY

It was 1944 and the Weiss family had been persecuted and stripped of their belongings; so far they had escaped being sent to the Nazi camps but Eva's father decided he must send his children into hiding. Two of them, Kurt and Neomi, had already been sent to a place in the mountains and the two youngest were hidden in another city.

Eva and Marta were waiting to catch a train to Nitra to stay with a German nurse who would be paid to care for them. They had false papers saying they were the nurse's sisters.

Eva's father took her small face in his hands. She was 12 years old and the eldest of his daughters.

'You are on your own now, Eva. But we can still keep in touch by looking at the stars each night. Whenever you are hurt or afraid, look at the stars. I will be looking at the stars too. I will listen, I will hear you and answer.'

As she stepped onto the train, Eva looked back at her father. His face was tired and drawn. He had worked hard helping the last of the Jewish people living in Bratislava, Czechoslovakia. Eva would cling to the memory of those last words with her father.

SISTERS TOGETHER

Despite all their father's careful planning, the girls were not safe for long. Suspicious neighbours reported them to the police. The nurse betrayed them, and the girls were sent to Auschwitz. They spent seven days packed into a railway wagon, with people dying of hunger and thirst around them before they reached the death camp. When the train stopped, someone hoisted Marta up so she could see through the grille at the railway yard.

'There are big chimneys with smoke coming out of them, and fences with barbed wire, and lots of guards and towers,' cried Marta.

'Come with us,' said some older children to Eva. 'You can pass for sixteen if you stand up straight. You will be safe if you come with us. If you stay with your little sister, you are doomed.'

'I can't make a choice like that,' said Eva.

'Listen to them, Eva. You must go,' said Marta. 'I can die by myself. You live. Just remember this day and say Kaddish [a memorial prayer] for me. Tell Mama and Papa too – so they can say Kaddish too. You must live.'

But as Eva turned to go, Marta tugged her skirt. 'I'm frightened,' she said softly.

Eva looked at the small girl and took a breath.

'I won't leave you. From now on we'll never be apart,' she said.

Eva kept her promise to Marta. Even though they were starved, beaten and tortured, Marta and Eva managed to stay together.

They were taken to the children's camp, where all night the sound of children crying echoed through the barracks. And every night, though Eva thought it might be her last, she spoke to her father through the stars. She told him what was happening to her – of her fears, her worries, of the unspeakably cruel things that were done to the children in the death camp.

DEATH AND REMEMBRANCE

Every day, groups of children were rounded up to be taken away for horrific medical experiments. Many of them never returned. One day, a five-year-old boy turned to Eva as he was about to be led away.

'Please remember today and say Kaddish after me,' he whispered, knowing that he was about to die.

'But I don't know what date it is!' she cried. 'I have to know what day it is to say Kaddish for you.'

The boy's face crumpled with distress. Eva reached out to him, and suddenly she saw the number that the Germans had tattooed into the flesh of her arm. Every member of the camp, even the children, had been branded with a number to identify them.

'You know what?' she said. 'My number will be your Kaddish.'

The boy looked back at Eva and smiled as he was led away. Eva bowed her head and prayed for him.

THE COURAGE OF LOVE

When the Russians finally liberated the camp, they talked of taking all the children back to Russia with them.

Terrified, Eva and Marta ran away. They were determined to get back to their parents.

It took months of travelling through war-torn Poland and Czechoslovakia to reach Bratislava again. Eva and Marta arrived back in their home town on a Sabbath morning. As they reached the gate of their house, their father and brother were returning from the synagogue. Even though Eva's head had been shaved, even though she was little more than a skeleton, her father knew her immediately.

Eva's family took her to live in Australia in 1948. When she grew up, she married, had five children of her own and tried to rebuild what had been lost. Yet though more than 70 years have passed, Eva still says Kaddish for the small boy who was murdered in Auschwitz.

For many years, Eva found it too hard to talk about the terrible things that happened to her, but eventually she courageously wrote a book about her experiences, even though the memories were so painful. The book *Gazing at the Stars: Memories of a Child Survivor* was published in 2014.

Even when remembering hurts, it's important to honour those who suffered by telling their stories. If we keep remembering, maybe we can make sure the worst things never happen again.

Although six million European Jews died in the death camps during the war, some escaped. Some managed to leave Europe, some stayed in hiding and some joined partisan movements and fought back against the Nazis.

FREIGHT TRAIN AT OPATOVA

'Twelve minutes,' said Batko. 'It takes twelve minutes from when we hear them to when they reach the bend. That's how long we have to set it up. Paul, you can be my helper for this one.'

'Yes sir,' said Paul, swallowing hard. Paul Strassmann was 15 years old and this was his first mission with the local partisans, near Trencin in Slovakia. They were a tough group of men who sabotaged the Nazis, and Batko was their leader.

'The trick is to blow just one section of the track, right on the bend,' continued Batko. 'If we do it properly, it will derail the whole train and drag it down the embankment. Maximum damage with minimum fuss.'

All day, they lay on the hill and watched the freight trains, laden with German soldiers, pass along the line. They were waiting for the cover of darkness so they could get to work. By evening, rain was pouring down. While the other men covered them with rifles, Batko and Paul crossed a flat muddy field and hid in a ditch under the rail embankment, listening hard. The rain was so heavy it would muffle the sound of the approaching train. They wouldn't have 12 minutes to mine the line – more like five. Batko placed two boxes of the explosive TNT under the rails and linked the cords to the TNT.

'Detonators,' he said.

Paul opened the thick leather pouch he wore at his waist. Nestled in the soft cotton padding were more than a dozen copper detonators. He drew out two caps and set them in place.

'Okay Paul, now we run,' said Batko as the sound of the train grew louder. Paul spun around to follow him, and the contents of the pouch scattered onto the ground – he had forgotten to shut it properly. His heart sank. Without the caps, there would be no more chances to blow up the lines – this was their entire supply. With the lights of the engine bearing down on him, he scrambled around in the rain, shoving the caps into his pockets, then he picked up his rifle and ran.

Paul stumbled down the embankment and onto the open muddy field that lay between the railway line and the forest. Fifty metres from the line he realised the train was about to pass over the detonators. He threw himself down in the sticky grey mud. As he fell, the TNT blew. Shards of metal flew over his head, some of them digging their jagged edges into the mud around him. Paul looked back over his shoulder to see the entire front of the train lurching down the embankment. He could feel the vibrations of crunching metal as the rear railcars slammed against the wreck of the front carriage.

Paul leaped to his feet and ran again. A bright white flare exploded overhead, and bullets whizzed around his head as the Germans opened fire on the field with machine guns. Paul dived back down into the mud. When the flare burned out, he was up and running, a moving lump of mud.

Finally, he met up with the squad in the forest. 'Where's that Jewish kid who had my detonators?' Batko was roaring. He was pulling his revolver out of its holster. 'He lost the lot, every last detonator, I saw the pouch fly open. I'm gonna get rid of that kid.'

Paul stepped forward, unrecognisable in his shroud of mud. Silently, he plunged his hand into his pocket and pulled out a fistful of detonators. Batko blinked and leaped backwards. The whole squad dived for cover. One squeeze of the caps and Paul would blow himself sky-high.

Suddenly, Batko laughed. 'Okay, kid – you live again,' he said.

Paul became an expert in derailing trains and an essential member of Batko's demolition squad. After the war, he went to live in the United States, where he studied engineering and eventually became a consultant to NASA.

Thousands of kids across Europe escaped to the woods, like Paul, and joined the partisan groups. They lived in the forests making their camps among the trees, covering their tracks wherever they went. Every day they worked at blowing up bridges, derailing troop trains, cutting communication wires or nursing other partisans – the faces of those they had lost always before them.

After the war, some Holocaust survivors returned to their home towns. Some went to America, Australia, Israel and other countries to make new lives for themselves, but every year, on

the anniversary of the deaths of their friends and family, they light candles. As long as people have the courage to remember the dark past and light a candle, there is hope.

PIRATES AND SWINGERS

It's hard to believe that anyone could have supported Hitler, but millions of people did. Hitler ordered every German child to join youth clubs. The kids wore brown uniforms and participated in events to support the Nazi Party. But not everyone wanted to join.

Most of the Edelweiss Pirates were aged between 14 and 18 years of age, but some of them were as young as 12. They made up their own uniform and wore little metal flowers on their collars, a skull and crossbones, a checked shirt, dark short trousers and white stockings. There were gangs in most major cities in Germany, and every one of them resisted the efforts of the government to turn them into Nazis.

The Edelweiss Pirates hated Hitler and the youth clubs that were organised in his name. Eternal War on the Hitler Youth was their motto. The Nazis tried to break up the gangs, but as soon as the ringleaders were arrested more boys took their place. As the war dragged on, the Pirates made as much trouble as they could. Brawls between the Pirates and the Hitler Youth League were common. In 1944, 16-year-old Bartholomäus Schink was hanged as ringleader of the Cologne Pirates. Finally, thousands of the Pirates were rounded up and sent to camps.

Kids who were into jazz music hated the Nazis too. They

called themselves Swing Kids. They jived, jitterbugged, listened to music from England and America, and welcomed Jewish kids into their clubs. Many of them wound up in camps as well.

Despite the threat of death, thousands of kids did what they thought was right – not what they were told. Sometimes with their parents' help, sometimes on their own, they helped Jewish people and tried to right what wrongs they could. The next story is about two kids who risked their lives for what they knew was right.

COURAGE

Helena Pódgorska sat up in the bed she shared with her big sister.

'Stefania, wake up,' she said, shaking her. 'I think there is someone knocking at the back door.'

It was 1941 and apart from one woman, Stefania and Helena were the only two people left in the big apartment building. The year before, the building had been full of Jewish families, but since the Germans had invaded Poland all the Jewish people had been forced to move into a ghetto. A third of the people in Przemysl – over 17 000 – were Jewish, and yet now they were all forced to live in a tiny area while the rest of the city felt empty.

At night, the girls heard terrible screams from the ghetto. Helena was only six, but she understood that there was good reason to be afraid of someone knocking on your door in the middle of the night.

'Who is it?' called Stefania.

'It's Max.'

'Max who?'

'Max Diamant. You worked for my mother.'

Stefania had been 13 when she went to live with the Diamants and they had taken her in as one of the family. Max, ten years older than Stefania, had treated her as if she was his kid sister. Stefania had worked happily in Mrs Diamant's grocery shop for three years – until the Diamants were sent to the Jewish ghetto.

Stefania flung the door open and Max staggered over the threshold. His face and hands were covered in blood, his clothes were torn and he could barely stand up.

'Please, Stefania, I need shelter. Just for tonight.'

'Of course, Max, but first we must clean you up,' she said. 'Helena, let's heat some water and get some cloths so we can dress these wounds.'

Together Stefania and Helena cleaned Max and put ointment on his countless scratches and bruises.

'I slipped under the fence of the ghetto today to visit you but I couldn't find anyone,' said Stefania as she wiped the blood from his face. 'What has happened?'

'They've all been murdered or deported to the camps, Stefania. My brother Henek and I, when they came to take us, we made a pact that we would commit suicide by jumping off the train. I wanted to die, Stefania, but I am alive thanks to you.'

'Me?' exclaimed Stefania.

'Yes, you. That loaf of bread you gave me the last time you visited – I put it inside my shirt. When I jumped from the car I saw a telegraph pole with a long spike sticking out rushing towards me. I thought, *Right, this is it,* and I blacked out. But when I came to I was lying on the ground, my shirt had a big tear in it, and the bread was torn open. I think I broke a little bone in my chest but that is all. Your bread saved my life.'

Stefania began to cry.

'Oh Max,' she said, 'I couldn't save your brother Isaac.'

Max went pale.

Stefania took his hand and told her story. After Mr and Mrs Diamant had been sent to Auschwitz, Max's brother Isaac was sent to the labour camp in nearby Lvov. Stefania went to visit him and together they dreamt up a harebrained plan. Isaac would dress in clothes that Stefania would smuggle in to him and wait by the side of the camp. At an appointed time, Stefania was to stand on the nearest corner. Isaac would scale the fence and run to her.

'If you are with me, we can just disappear into the crowd,' said Stefania. 'If anyone asks, I will say you are my brother.'

But the trolley-car Stefania was travelling on was held up.

'I was so late. I was too late,' wept Stefania. 'When I got to the camp, they told me he was dead. He saw a woman that looked like me and ran to her, and she turned him over to the police. I am so sorry, Max. I came to tell you, but when I got back to the ghetto everyone was gone!'

Max looked pale and exhausted. He rested one hand on Stefania's shoulder.

'You tried, Stefania. You are a brave girl, my friend. You risked your life. Now you risk it again. No one else will take me in. They are too afraid. All my friends have turned me away. If you could let me stay just this one night, maybe tomorrow I will have the strength to search for a hiding place.'

Stefania nodded in mute agreement.

Max's clothes were bloodied and torn, so Stefania lent him some of her clothes. Little Helena clapped her hands and laughed when Max emerged from the bedroom in one of Stefania's long flannel nightgowns.

'Now I see two Stefanias!' she giggled, and the three of them laughed.

THE HIDING PLACE

The next day Max was too sick to leave. Helena had to be the scout who would listen to hear if anyone was coming, especially the other woman who lived in the building. She would run into the bedroom and help Stefania hide Max under the bed.

The girls got used to hiding Max and when he brought a friend, Danuta, back with him they didn't hesitate to take her in too. Soon Max's other brother, Henek, who had also survived leaping from the train, joined them as well.

Stefania and Helena worked hard to help their Jewish friends. Stefania had a job in a factory and used all the money she could spare to buy food for Max and Danuta to smuggle into the ghetto. She even traded her dresses for milk and butter.

One night, Max told Stefania the ghetto was about to be completely destroyed. They agreed they must try to rescue as many people as they could, but how? There was no more room in the apartment to hide anyone.

Stefania knew she had to find somewhere else for them all

to live. The task seemed daunting, but a voice inside her told her she would succeed. By a miracle she found exactly what they needed – a cottage with two rooms in the front and rear and a big attic. Helena rolled around the floor and laughed with joy when Stefania took her to look at the cottage.

'It's perfect,' exclaimed Helena. 'We can hide everyone here!'

By the time Helena turned seven, there were six Jewish friends to sing her happy birthday, including two children.

When Stefania's Jewish friends asked her if she was afraid, she said, 'They can only kill us once for hiding Jews, not ten times. As long as we can fit more people in, we may as well.' Helena nodded in agreement.

Together they came up with a plan to smuggle the two fathers of the children already in their care out of the ghetto. The plan was to have a postman guide them – but on the day the men were to arrive at the cottage, a group of German and Polish policemen began patrolling the street.

'Perhaps today is the day I will be killed,' thought Stefania.

Stefania went to the church and prayed. When she came home, the fathers had arrived safely. Luckily, the postman had got lost on the way to Stefania's house and he was so late that the policemen had left by the time he arrived.

EATING WORDS

Helena grew used to passing notes between Stefania and the last of the Jews in the ghetto. The small girl would slip under the barbed wire when no one was watching. But one day, a gang of teenage boys saw Helena and chased her.

Helena couldn't read or write, but she knew the message she carried spelled trouble for all the Jewish people they were hiding. As she ran, she tore the paper into little pieces and ate it – piece by piece. By the time the boys caught up with her she had swallowed the whole note.

'What were you doing in there?' they said. 'Show us what's in your hands.'

Silently Helena held them out, empty.

'Turn her pockets out,' ordered the ringleader.

The boys slapped Helena as she struggled but still she said nothing.

'Rotten little Jew-lover,' they shouted, ripping the pockets off the front of her dress. They beat her and kicked her so badly that she could barely struggle home.

'I told them nothing, Stefania. I told them nothing,' she said as she fell into her sister's arms.

Helena had trained herself so well never to betray the people she was protecting that she became mute for four years after the war ended, and for the rest of her life she spoke with a stutter.

FULL HOUSE

As the last of the Jews of Przemysl were rounded up and sent to death camps, Stefania and Helena took in seven more people. Now they had 13 Jewish men, women and children living in the attic of their cottage. Together, they built a false wall in the attic so they could all hide behind it in an emergency.

Stefania worked in a factory. There was so much food needed to feed 15 people. When she turned 17, her employers put her wages up just a little bit, but no matter how hard she worked, she could never earn enough to feed them all properly.

Seven-year-old Helena managed the house on her own during the day and did all the shopping. If anyone asked her how two girls could eat so much food, Helena would tell the shopkeepers that she was selling the extra loaves of bread and sacks of potatoes on the black market. Because of the war, food, medicine, cigarettes and many other things were in short supply across Europe. Shopkeepers were forced to keep their prices reasonable but many people engaged in an illegal (black) market, reselling ordinary goods at high prices to be shipped to areas where the goods were scarce.

After three years – towards the end of the war – a field hospital for the Germans opened in the building opposite Stefania and Helena's cottage. Soldiers came and ordered the sisters to leave. The cottage was to be used to house members of the military.

For two hours, Stefania ran frantically through Przemysl looking for a house where she could hide her 13 friends, but she could find nothing. She gave up and returned to the cottage.

'Run away, don't die with us,' said Max. 'You cannot help us any more – you have done what you could. Save your life and save Helena.'

'No,' said Helena. 'No, we can't go.'

Stefania looked from her sister to her friends. 'We won't go. We will pray,' said Stefania. As she prayed, her inner voice spoke to her again and told her to be strong and calm.

'Everything will be all right,' said Stefania as she rose to her feet. 'Hide in the attic. Our prayers will be answered.'

Stefania and Helena went downstairs and flung all the windows wide open.

'Miss Pódgorska! What are you and your sister doing here?' said her neighbours.

'We're staying. We refuse to be moved,' she replied. 'I'm sick of being shifted around!'

'You're crazy!' said her neighbours. 'They'll kill you both.'

Stefania shrugged. 'We won't go, whatever they do.'

Helena and Stefania cleaned the house, singing all the time. Against all odds, when an SS officer came to inspect the house he said it was all right for them to stay. The army only wanted one room for two nurses to live in.

The nurses moved in and their German soldier boyfriends came and visited them nearly every night. Every night for eight months the nurses and soldiers slept directly under the attic that hid 13 Jews. Every morning, Stefania and Helena watched the German soldiers pick up their guns and wondered if today was the day that they would all be shot.

But the Russian army was moving closer to Przemysl, driving the German army out of Poland and time was running out for the Germans. Eventually, the field hospital had to pack up and move on and the nurses and their soldier boyfriends departed.

LIBERATION

Finally, Russian soldiers came to liberate Przemysl from the Germans. Two soldiers came to Stefania's door, trying to trade chocolate for vodka. Stefania eyed them suspiciously.

'Where are the Germans?' she asked.

'You sound like a spy,' replied the soldiers. 'But look, we've already chased the Germans away. They're never coming back.'

Suddenly, the Jews burst into the room, weeping with relief. They had overheard the Russian soldiers' conversation. The Russians reached for their guns in alarm.

'Don't worry, these are my friends,' cried Stefania. 'Jewish friends. Helena and I have kept them hidden for three years. They are quiet people, good people, the best of people. Please, put your guns away.'

The soldiers gazed at the girls in disbelief.

'Two girls!' said one of the soldiers.

'Not even two,' said the other, looking at little Helena and laughing. 'Just a girl and a half!'

Thirteen people, their kids and their grandkids are alive today because two girls had big hearts, a tonne of courage and believed in miracles.

EVER AFTER

After the war, Stefania married Max Diamant. Max changed his name to Josef Burzminski and in 1961 the couple immigrated to the USA, where they raised two children and lived for the rest of their lives. Helena remained in Poland and became a doctor.

In 1996, a movie – *Hidden in Silence* – was made of Stefania's story. Josef (Max) died in 2003 and Stefania in 2017, but their story of love and friendship continues to inspire people. When Stefania was interviewed about those long and difficult years of hiding her friends she said, 'I want people to know about helping one another, not to kill but just to be human beings. People should learn to live together.'

CLIMATE WARRIORS

SAVING THE PLANET, PROTECTING THE FUTURE

The world is always changing but in the last 40 years climate change has alarmed scientists around the world. Every year, global temperatures have risen and the 12 warmest years ever recorded have all occurred since 1998. As the planet warms, the impact on the sea and land endangers all living creatures. In addition, modern technology has generated new levels of pollution and the earth is struggling to cope with Its impact.

Scientists aren't the only ones who are worried about global warming and pollution. Kids have taken up the battle cry to save the planet. All over the world, children have come together to fight for their future. They don't need guns to win the battle, they just need courage.

In the USA, 21 young people between the ages of 11 and 22 years are suing their government for failing to protect the Earth, and the children, from the effects of climate change.

In Columbia, 25 children and young people led a court action to have the Columbian Amazon rainforest declared 'a person' to protect its legal rights and prevent its destruction. The kids accused the government of failing to protect the forests and the children's right to a healthy environment and they won.

The kids in this chapter have each looked at the world around them and realised that they can make a difference. Each of them is a beacon of hope for a better future for us all.

OCEAN BOY

Greece, 2010

Sixteen-year-old Boyan Slat slipped on his mask and dived under the surface of the sparkling waters of the Mediterranean Sea. When he was at home in Delft, in the Netherlands, it took half an hour to drive to the North Sea and the water there was often freezing, so Boyan was thrilled to be on school holidays in the Greek Islands. He'd been looking forward to scuba diving, but as Boyan swam further from the shore he started to feel uneasy. Where were all the fish? And why was there so much plastic scattered across the seabed and floating all around him?

When Boyan surfaced, he found his diving companion treading water. 'There surely is a lot of jellyfish down there!' joked the Scottish diver, referring to the hundreds of plastic bags floating in the sea.

Boyan shook his head. It made him feel both sad and angry. How could there be more plastic bags than fish?

When Boyan returned to school after the holidays, he decided to do a school project on the problem of plastic in the oceans. He discovered that there were five different areas in the world's oceans where rubbish collects. Ocean currents carry plastic and other waste to these five areas, which are called 'gyres'. They're also called the 'ocean garbage patches', and they are huge. The gyres spread across millions of square kilometres and stretch in every direction. The largest patch is called the Great Pacific Garbage Patch and lies between Hawaii and the city of San Francisco in California. It's nearly as big as the whole state of Queensland in Australia (which is twice the size of France). It covers 1.6 million square kilometres and contains an estimated 1.8 trillion pieces of plastic that weigh as much as 43 000 cars!

What surprised Boyan the most as he read about the Great Pacific Garbage Patch was that no one was doing anything about it, or any of the other four ocean gyres. He realised the plastic wasn't going to go away unless someone cleaned it up.

FROM ROCKETS TO RESEARCH

Boyan Slat loved engineering. He'd loved it from when he was two years old and first began trying to understand how machines worked. All through his childhood, Boyan tinkered with making things – from treehouses to zip-lines to rockets. In June 2009, when Boyan was 14, he had organised an event with other kids in Delft that would set a Guinness World Record: they simultaneously launched 213 water rockets on a sports field of the Delft University of Technology.

Boyan was so fascinated by rockets that when he finished

high school he enrolled at the University of Delft to study aerospace engineering. But even though he loved the idea of being an aerospace engineer, he'd never stopped worrying about the problem of plastics in the oceans. In his last two years of high school, he'd spent countless hours researching the problem and puzzling over how it could be solved. It kept him awake at night, but he kept experimenting with designs for an engineering solution that would help catch all the plastics in the oceans so that they could be recycled.

It didn't take long for Boyan to realise that using ships with nets would cost a fortune and probably be harmful to sea life. One scientist suggested it would take 79 000 years to clean up the mess using conventional methods. Ships with nets would have to travel a huge distance across the gyres and would emit enormous amounts of carbon, adding to world air pollution.

After experimenting with different types of filters and devices, Boyan came up with the idea of using the ocean currents to help concentrate the garbage into a smaller area. If he could somehow fix a zigzag array of solar platforms with a long floating boom stretched between them in the gyres, the boom could trap the garbage and make it much easier to collect. Fish and sea life would swim unharmed under the boom.

DROPPING OUT AND GETTING STARTED

The more Boyan worked on his idea, the more he realised that no one else was doing anything. Boyan decided he couldn't wait for someone else to fix the problem. After discussing it with his parents, he dropped out of university and began to pour all his energy into solving the issue of plastic pollution in the world oceans.

The first challenge Boyan had to face was how to make enough money to do everything he dreamt of. By the time he was 18 he had saved up 300 euros ($470 Australian dollars), which was just enough to register his new organisation, The Ocean Clean-up. Next, he wrote to hundreds of companies asking for their help, but few of them replied and those that did told him his idea was terrible.

Then in 2012, he gave a TEDx talk about his ambition to clean the ocean. He looked like a floppy-haired high-school student, but when he spoke, everyone realised his message was important. The video was eventually picked up by other websites and it went viral. Millions of people watched it and Boyan began to receive donations from all over the world. Using crowdfunding, Boyan raised millions of dollars so that he could employ more scientists and engineers and start experimenting on how to make a large-scale version of his idea.

In September 2018, after five years of research and expeditions, the first 600-metre floating 'garbage-catcher' was put on a ship at San Francisco and taken to the Great Pacific Garbage Patch to begin its work.

In the first three months, the system collected two metric tonnes of 'ghost nets' – fishing nets that have been lost or discarded by fishermen. The nets are mostly made of plastic and are dangerous to sea life. Although the floating boom had a three metre 'skirt' attached to it to help trap smaller pieces of plastic, the small pieces failed to stay in the boom. It was a disappointing result but Boyan and his team got back to work, designing improvements to the system. When part of the boom broke, the Ocean Cleanup team was forced to return the entire system to port for repairs and improvements to its design. Once the first model is perfected, Boyan intends to send 120 of the garbage catchers into the five gyres to gather up all the floating plastics. His aim is to catch 90 per cent of ocean plastics by 2040. He hopes that the clean-up will eventually pay for itself by recycling the collected plastics, and his organisation is working hard on researching ways to make this possible.

ACCOLADES FOR OCEAN BOY

Boyan has received many awards and grants, publicity and praise, as well as criticism, for his work. Some people have said the money he has raised for the project would be better spent on other initatives. The United Nations Environment Programme recognised his work with a Champions of the Earth award, but for Boyan, the greatest reward of all will be when he has fulfilled his life mission and the oceans he loves so much are free of plastics. It may take a lifetime, but he is determined to see it happen.

A MESS OF MICRO PLASTICS

Every year, humans are responsible for the dumping of around 8 million metric tonnes of plastic into the oceans, where fish and mammals and birds mistake it for food. Red plastic often winds up being eaten by birds – and it kills them. Other sea life is also killed or horribly damaged. Plastics slowly break down into tiny micro plastics that are impossible to remove from the environment. The micro plastics can poison water, too, so as well as cleaning up the mess, the people of the world need to stop using so much plastic and definitely stop throwing it away.

While Boyan Slat was busy planning how to scoop plastic from the ocean, two girls on the other side of the planet were trying to think up ways to stop it getting into the water in the first place.

MAKING A DIFFERENCE

Ubud, Bali, 2013

The air shimmered in the afternoon heat. Ten-year-old Isabel Wijsen tipped her head to one side and listened closely as her teacher spoke about the famous African political activist, Nelson Mandela, and the Indian peace activist, Mahatma Gandhi. Isabel's big sister, 12-year-old Melati, was in the class too, listening to stories about people through history who had been a force for good. Then the teacher asked the students to think about what *they* might do to make a difference.

Isabel and Melati attended The Green School near the Ayung River in Ubud, in the heart of Bali. It's an unusual school, built from bamboo poles and set in a tropical jungle-like environment. Isabel and Melati both had a lot to think about as they left their classroom that day.

As they walked home between the rice fields, Isabel glanced across at Melati.

'I wish we could do something. Why do we have to wait until we're grown up?' asked Isabel.

'Just because we're kids doesn't mean we can't do something to help the world right now,' said Melati.

'But what can we change?' asked Isabel.

'There's something that I'd like to change,' said Melati, pointing at all the plastic that was littered along the pathway. 'All that plastic garbage – it's terrible. Remember at the beach last weekend? There was so much plastic everywhere, it was floating around us while we were swimming – plastic bags and bottles and straws. Ugh!'

'It's horrible,' said Isabel. 'I hate the way it clogs the gutters whenever it rains and then it winds up in the rivers. It's ugly and it's dangerous to animals and fish.'

Melati stopped and looked at her sister.

'Are you thinking what I'm thinking?' said Melati. 'I mean, you hate plastic, I hate it too. Everyone in Bali hates trash. Maybe we could start now, right here, making a difference in our own home.'

BYE BYE PLASTIC BAGS

Isabel and Melati's mother was from Holland and their father was from Java, in Indonesia, but the two girls had been born in Bali and had grown up there. They loved how lush and beautiful their home was and they were proud that it was often called the Island of the Gods. But they had watched the increasing problem of mountains of plastic grow worse each year of their lives.

That evening, as the sisters sat on a couch in their home, listening to the calls of the night birds and the buzz of insects, they talked about how they might keep their island home beautiful. The girls didn't know then that their plan for their own island would wind up becoming an international movement. But they were clear that if there was one thing that could make a big difference to the environment in Bali, it would be getting rid of plastic bags. Isabel and Melati decided to call their new organisation Bye Bye Plastic Bags.

Plastic pollution is an international problem. Denmark was the first country to try and limit plastic bags by introducing a levy, or extra price, on them in 1993. In 2008, Rwanda, in Africa, became the first country in the world to introduce a complete ban on plastic bags. Some countries have extra taxes on plastics, and some have none. In 2017 the city of Delhi in India, which has over 20 million people, not only banned single-use plastic bags but introduced a fine for people caught using them.

Isabel and Melati did some research into plastic bag pollution, but they knew that they couldn't start a movement for change all by themselves. So the girls organised a crew of other kids to help with the plan, and they began brainstorming ideas for how they could make their vision of a plastic-bag-free Bali a reality.

Their first attempt to get the government of Bali to support their plan wasn't very successful. No one from the government wanted to talk to a bunch of children.

In October 2013, Bye Bye Plastic Bags launched a giant petition calling for a ban on plastic bags in Bali. Isabel and Melati and their friends promoted their petition on the internet and also asked everyone they knew to sign. Then they appealed to the airport in Denpasar to let them ask for signatures from everyone arriving in or leaving Bali. It took them some time to convince the authorities to let a team of children hang out in the terminal asking for signatures, but eventually they got permission. The children collected over 10 000 signatures at the airport and elsewhere, in addition to collecting 770 000 online, then they presented their petition to the Governor of Bali.

The following year they began to spread their message even further, giving talks in other schools and creating a booklet about the damage plastic can do, how to use less plastic and solutions for plastic pollution. They also gave away alternative bags to all sorts of shops and small roadside sellers so that they wouldn't need to use plastic bags.

GOING GLOBAL

Despite endless letters, emails and phone calls, the Governor of Bali refused to meet with the children from Bye Bye Plastic Bags. But after Isabel and Melati visited India with their parents in 2014, they came up with a new plan. In India, they heard about how Mahatma Gandhi went on a hunger strike to make the British Government listen to his plea to make India an independent country. Isabel and Melati decided they, too, would give up eating until the Governor of Bali agreed to see them.

As the girls were still only 11 and 13 years old, their parents weren't very happy with the plan. As a compromise, Isabel and Melati went to see a nutritionist and then agreed that they would eat nothing from sunrise to sunset but would eat planned meals as long as it was dark. When the Governor heard that the girls were refusing food, he finally agreed to meet with them. In the meeting, he committed to help the girls rid Bali of plastic bags.

But the following year, Bali still produced 680 cubic metres of plastic garbage a day. Isabel and Melati knew they couldn't stop campaigning. They published their booklet, and launched a new campaign called One Island, One Voice, encouraging shops to declare themselves Plastic-Bag-Free-Zones. Later that year, the Governor signed a letter announcing that Bali would be plastic free by 2018. Finally, the girls felt they were getting somewhere.

Isabel and Melati gave a talk on TED, and before long more than a million people had watched it. People all around the world became interested in their campaign. Bye Bye Plastic Bags became a global force, with other young people setting up their own branches of the organisation in over 20 different countries.

By 2017, the girls' One Island, One Voice campaign had been joined by other organisations across Bali. Together they organised a huge clean-up of the island – Bali's Biggest Beach Clean Up. Twelve thousand people collected nearly 40 tonnes of garbage in 55 different places across Bali. There had never been a clean-up like it in the history of Bali, but in 2018 they did it again. Twenty thousand people joined the clean-up this time and removed close to 65 tonnes of garbage. In addition to the clean-ups, they started other projects too, including placing booms in the rivers to catch plastic before it reached the ocean. The word was spreading about all their good work; the force was growing but there was still much, much more to do.

At the end of 2018, the Governor of Bali announced that from 1 January 2019, single use plastic bags, Styrofoam and plastic straws would be banned in Denpasar, Bali's capital city. After five years of campaigning the announcement was a win for a cleaner

Bali, but the Wijsen sisters and their team are determined to make *all* of Bali plastic bag free. As Isabel has often said, 'Kids might be only twenty-five per cent of the world's population, but they are one hundred per cent of the future.'

THE LITTLEST CLIMATE WARRIOR

Felix Finkbeiner loved polar bears. Even though he lived in Pähl, a small town in Bavaria in the south of Germany, he felt connected to the majestic white bears of the Arctic. He'd always thought of them as his favourite animal. But then his teacher asked him to do a project on global warming and everything he imagined about polar bears was turned upside down.

On a cold January evening in 2007, Felix sat down at the family computer and read about how the Arctic, the home of the polar bears, is warming twice as fast as anywhere else on Earth. Felix felt a stab of fear. He began searching for more information on the internet and noticed that a woman called Wangari Maathai kept appearing in his searches. Felix was nine years old and had never heard of the Kenyan woman who, along with other women in Kenya, had planted 30 million trees in 30 years in Africa. It seemed incredible that one woman could be responsible for so much good.

A few days later, when Felix stood at the front of his class to begin his presentation, he felt a little nervous. He pushed his wire-rimmed glasses into place and brushed his fringe to one side. He'd never felt as strongly about anything as he did about this talk on global warming. What he had read on the internet had frightened him; and when Felix was frightened, he knew it meant he had to be brave. If Wangari Maathai could achieve so much with so little, surely he and his friends could do something too.

'The ice caps in the Arctic are melting,' said Felix. 'That means that polar bears are in danger. If they lose their home, we will lose the polar bear. But it's not just about polar bears, it's about human beings too. We are all contributing to the warming of the Earth.

'When we burn fossil fuels like oil, coal and natural gas to make electricity, to heat our homes and to drive cars, we release carbon dioxide into the atmosphere,' explained Felix. 'Carbon dioxide causes global warming. But did you know that a single tree can absorb ten kilograms of carbon dioxide every year? Trees capture carbon dioxide so one way to help slow climate change is to plant trees.'

Then he described the work of Wangari Maathai.

'We have to do the same,' he said. 'We have to be like Wangari Maathai.'

When Felix finished his speech, he felt fired up and so did his classmates. Along with his friends, Felix started a new organisation dedicated to planting trees, Plant-for-the-Planet. Felix vowed that with the help of the other children he would plant one million trees before he grew up.

THE FIRST TREE

Two months later, on 28 March 2007, Felix planted his first tree near the front gate of his school in Starnberg. It was a small crabapple tree that his mother had bought to help Felix get his campaign underway. Felix had already begun writing to other kids at other schools in Bavaria, asking them to join Plant-for-the-Planet. As more and more children joined, they brought different skills to the campaign. Some helped Felix to build a website; other kids spread the word to more schools in their region. Soon the story of the children who were planting trees began to spread across Germany.

In April 2008, just over a year after planting his first tree, Felix announced at a press conference that Plant-for-the-Planet had already planted 50 000 trees. Felix became so busy that it was hard for him to keep up with all the requests for information. His mother, Karolin, had always said if his grades began to fall, he'd have to pull back on his campaign. Felix asked his parents, 'If we got money to employ someone to help, could we do that?'

Not long after the conversation with his parents, Felix gave a talk at a local Rotary Club meeting. In the audience was the Chief Executive Officer of the car company, Toyota. After listening to Felix's impassioned speech, the CEO offered to form a partnership with Plant-for-the-Planet. As part of Toyota's 'green action' plan, the company would pay 40 000 euros so the children of Plant-for-the-Planet could have a full-time employee.

In the summer of 2008, Felix travelled to Norway to attend the United Nations Children's Conference where he was elected to the junior board of the UN Environment Programme (UNEP).

By November 2008, people from all across Germany had heard of Felix. So many people were interested in his ideas that he was invited to present to the European Parliament in Brussels about his work and his thoughts on climate justice. Felix told the grown-ups of the parliament that children, youth and adults all need to work together to solve the problems of the planet.

The following year, Felix spread his message even further when he flew to South Korea to present at a UNEP conference. Felix invited all the children from other countries to set up their own Plant-for-the-Planet groups. When he called for the children who would promise to plant one million trees in their own countries to join him on stage, hundreds of children from 56 nations marched up the steps to the stage and stood beside him. Plant-for-the-Planet became a global movement.

Felix and the children started a campaign – 'Stop Talking. Start Planting.' – and enlisted the help of international celebrities and politicians to promote his idea. Thanks to the pester power of the children, it took only three years for one million new trees to be planted in Germany.

TOWARDS ONE TRILLION

The International Year of the Forests in 2011 was an important year for Felix. He was 13 years old and invited to present at the United Nations Assembly in New York City. Supported by his friends from Plant-for-the-Planet, Felix announced to the audience of grown-ups his plan for the children of the world to plant one trillion trees (one thousand times one billion!).

By the end of 2018, over 100 000 children around the world, inspired by Felix, were involved with Plant-for-the-Planet. Together they were responsible for the planting of over 15.2

billion trees in 190 nations. If the children reach their goal, it will mean there will be 150 trees for every person on earth. These trees could capture 25 per cent of all the carbon emissions that humans make every year. Combined with lowering pollution, the children and the trees could make the world safer for everyone.

In addition to planting trees, Felix and his friends are committed to protecting trees, too. Plant-for-the-Planet ambassadors train in one-day workshops to become climate justice ambassadors and activists in their own communities. Most of the children are between the ages of nine and 12. The children give presentations that explain the ability of trees to capture carbon dioxide and slow climate change.

Plant-for-the-Planet is established in six countries and young climate warriors have given presentations in 67 different countries. In countries where they don't have an official group of child ambassadors, they partner with environmental agencies to make sure trees get planted.

FELIX GROWS UP

In 2018, at the age 19, Felix became one of the youngest people in German history to receive the Order of Merit of the Federal Republic of Germany. Felix went on to study at the School of Oriental and African Studies in London so he could understand more about world history. He also studied Chinese. In 2019, he moved to Zurich in Switzerland where he conducts research into which regions of the world are best suited for tree-planting.

The small crabapple tree in the schoolyard in Starnberg looks a little forlorn, but it's an important symbol of the power of children to make a difference. Felix has said that if he'd known how important that single tree would become, he would have asked his mother to buy something majestic, like a fir tree. But perhaps the fact that it's a small tree shows how big things can grow from the seed of an idea. One tree alone might not mean much, but when kids work together, they can plant forests. As Felix Finkbeiner said in his speech to the United Nations in New York, 'One mosquito cannot do anything against a rhino, but a thousand mosquitoes can make a rhino change its direction.'

EVERY KID CAN

RESOURCES AND EXTRA READING

One book can never be long enough to tell the millions of inspiring true stories about courageous kids that exist in our world.

Each and every day, we all make decisions that shape our future, no matter what our age or where we live. The story of tomorrow is being written by people making choices today. When people decide to be courageous, to help each other and to work together, their actions and their stories can change the world for the better.

If you found any of the stories in this book made you feel fired up to get involved with helping others, there are many organisations that need you. Whether you want to work to save the planet or lend a helping hand to someone in need, or simply sing your own song and tell your own story, being a kid shouldn't stop you. The human rights organisation Amnesty International has a youth network with branches in secondary schools across Australia but you don't have to wait until you are in high school to sign up with other groups. You can find the organisations that were mentioned in this book on the internet. Below is a list of a few of them that work especially with children or have been founded by children.

Everyone is the hero of their own story and every kid has a chance to make a difference.

Plant-for-the-Planet – **plant-for-the-planet.org**

Bye Bye Plastic Bags – **byebyeplasticbags.org**

Operation Day's Work USA – **odw-usa.org**

WE Movement – **we.org/we-movement**

Code Like a Girl – **codelikeagirl.org**

The World's Children's Prize – **worldschildrensprize.org**

Technovation – **technovationchallenge.org**

INDEX

ACKNOWLEDGEMENTS

This book, originally conceived of in 1996 and published in 1999, owes thanks to many people. For their input, inspiration, help and guidance in the creation of the 1999 edition, I thank: Walter Rutowski, Sue Cutler, Sally Rogow, Ron Adams, Magnus Bergmar, Steven Vitto, Juliet O'Connor; David, William and Matthew Taft; Harry Harrison, Sarah Brenan, Rosalind Price, Martin Gilbert, Eva Fogelman, Paul Valent and Isaac Kowalski, and all the younger Harpers and Murrays who were children when I wrote the first edition and are now impressive adults.

For permission to tell their stories in the 1999 edition, I thank Eva (Weiss) Slonim and Ruby Hunter (now deceased). It was an honour to interview both women in 1998 and to update their stories to reflect their subsequent achievements.

It was a privilege to be able to revise and update each story and to add so many new ones. Thank you to my publisher, Susannah Chambers, for recognising that good stories will always find readers, and to Hilary Reynolds for her clarity.

Special thanks to Cassidy and Linda Strickland, Felix Finkbeiner, Gitanjali and Bharatni Rao, Ron Adams (again!), Emma Yang, and Melati and Isabel Wijsen and their team at Bye Bye Plastic Bags, for their generosity in sharing their stories with me.

ABOUT THE AUTHOR

Kirsty Murray was born in Melbourne, the middle child in a family of seven kids. By the time she was a teenager, she knew she wanted to be a professional writer but it took her many years to realise that the stories she had loved most as a kid were exactly the sort of stories she wanted to write. She is now a multi-award winning author of books for children and young adults. Her works include eleven novels as well as non-fiction, junior fiction, historical fiction, speculative fiction and picture books. Kirsty is an ambassador and advocate for many reading and writing initiatives and has been a writer-in-residence in schools and universities. She has also travelled Australia and the world to collect inspiring stories. Her three children and three stepchildren are all grown up now but her grandchildren, godchildren and many young friends continue to fascinate and inspire her with their energy and ideas. She loves books, libraries, bookshops, readers, writers, and especially stories about all kinds of kids.

THE CHILDREN OF THE WIND QUARTET

by Kirsty Murray

The Children of the Wind quartet tells the stories of four courageous young people, Bridie, Billy, Colm and Maeve, born many years apart. They are action-packed inter-linked stories, beginning in 1840s Ireland and ending in present-day Australia.

CHILDREN OF THE WIND
Book 1

Bridie's world is torn apart when her parents and baby brother die in the Great Hunger. She leaves Ireland, and strikes out alone to claim a life for herself in Australia, on the other side of the ocean.

CHILDREN OF THE WIND
Book 2

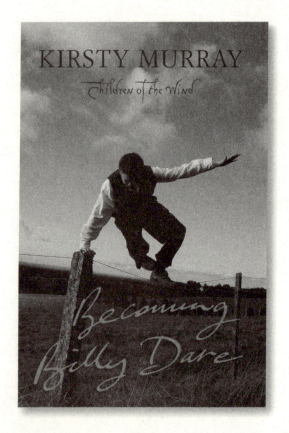

Paddy secretly boards a ship bound for Australia, only
to be shipwrecked at the end of the voyage. Once rescued,
he faces the big question: how is he to make his way
in this strange new land?

CHILDREN OF THE WIND
Book 3

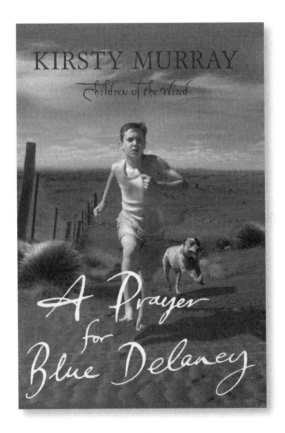

Colm is on the run, determined to escape from the cruelties of Bindoon Boys' Home. He strikes up an unexpected friendship with old Billy Dare and his dog Rusty, and together they travel from the goldfields of Kalgoorlie to the rugged north.

CHILDREN OF THE WIND
Book 4

KIRSTY MURRAY

The Secret Life of Maeve Lee Kwong

Maeve is devastated when her mother dies in a car crash.
Sent to live with her strict Chinese grandparents, she
fights to hold onto the things she loves most – her two
best friends, her dancing, her baby brother Ned – as she
searches for a path to follow, a place to belong.